Social Media for Home Builders, 2.0

Social Media for Home Builders 2.0

It's Easier Than You Think

Carol M. Flammer, CAPS, CSP, MIRM

National
Association
of Home
Builders

Social Media for Home Builders 2.0: It's Easier Than You Think
BuilderBooks, a Service of the National Association of Home Builders

Courtenay S. Brown	Director, Book Publishing
Natalie C. Holmes	Book Editor
Costin Marinescu	Cover Design
Circle Graphics	Composition
Sheridan Books, Inc.	Printing

Gerald M. Howard	NAHB Chief Executive Officer
Mark Pursell	NAHB Senior Vice President, Marketing & Sales Group
Lakisha Campbell	NAHB Vice President, Publishing & Affinity Programs

Disclaimer

This publication provides accurate information on the subject matter covered. The publisher is selling it with the understanding that the publisher is not providing legal, accounting, or other professional service. If you need legal advice or other expert assistance, obtain the services of a qualified professional experienced in the subject matter involved. Reference herein to any specific commercial products, process, or service by trade name, trademark, manufacturer, or otherwise does not necessarily constitute or imply its endorsement, recommendation, or favored status by the National Association of Home Builders. The views and opinions of the author expressed in this publication do not necessarily state or reflect those of the National Association of Home Builders, and they shall not be used to advertise or endorse a product.

Printed in the United States of America
15 14 13 12 11   1 2 3 4 5

Library of Congress Cataloging-in-Publication Data
Flammer, Carol M., 1967-
  Social media for home builders 2.0 : it's easier than you think / Carol M. Flammer.–
2nd ed. p. cm.
  Includes bibliographical references and index.
  ISBN 978-0-86718-675-8 (alk. paper)
  1. Internet marketing. 2. Social media–Marketing. 3. Construction industry–
Marketing. I. Title.
  HF5415.1265.F567 2011
  690.068 8–dc22
                2011009131

For further information, please contact:
National Association of Home Builders
1201 15th Street, NW
Washington, DC 20005-2800
800-223-2665
http://www.BuilderBooks.com

Contents

About the Author

Carol Flammer, MIRM, CAPS, CSP, has 20 years of experience as a public relations and *social media marketing* expert, strategist, and consultant. She is president of Flammer Relations, Inc., and managing partner of mRELEVANCE, LLC, an Internet marketing, social media, and public relations firm with offices in Atlanta and Chicago.

Carol is the creator of the nationally ranked and award-winning http://www.AtlantaRealEstateForum.com, an Atlanta real estate blog. She was blogging long before blogging was "cool."

Carol teaches seminars on social media through home builders associations (HBAs) nationwide and has spoken at numerous trade shows and conferences, including the International Builders' Show, REtechSouth, New Media Atlanta, and the Southern Building Show. She urges her audience to consider the question, "When you Google your name, do you like what you see?"

Carol holds a BA in Business and Behavioral Science from Oglethorpe University. A member of the Greater Atlanta HBA, Carol was honored in 2008 as Associate of the Year. She is a member of the Georgia Chapter of the Public Relations Society of America and a recipient of

PRSA's prestigious George Goodwin Award. Other recognitions include the Oglethorpe University 2008 Spirit of Oglethorpe Award, as well as OBIE, Phoenix, APEX, Hermes, and Communicator Awards for blogs and client projects.

Carol is a member of the Atlanta Apartment Association, Urban Land Institute, National Association of Real Estate Editors, and Professional Women in Building. She serves on the *Sales and Marketing Ideas* Editorial Advisory Committee and the Board of the Atlanta HBA's Sales and Marketing Council.

In her free time, Carol pursues her love of dressage. Read all about her Trakehner stallion Favian *Ps at http://www.TheBigRedHorse.com (yes, even her horse has a blog). She and her family live at their farm, Thistledown, in Cartersville, Georgia.

Foreword

October 29, 2005, is a day I will never forget. It was the day Blogging Systems, a company I served as marketing director, opened for business on the expo hall floor of the National Association of Realtors annual convention in San Francisco. Our company's sole focus was to bring business blogging to the real estate industry. Our $10' \times 10'$ trade show booth was inundated with agents and brokers who wanted to know how this new form of online communication could help their businesses. I am proud to say that the real estate industry has been a forerunner in the use of this new media.

Since then, social networking sites like Facebook and Twitter have become integral to our cultural landscape. At the same time, consumers have grown more skeptical of advertising and marketing claims that often overpromise and under-deliver. Instead, consumers trust each other to inform purchasing decisions, including the largest one most people will ever make–buying a home.

Consumers already may have engaged you in their online conversations. It makes perfect sense for home builders, real estate agents, mortgage professionals, and anyone else related to the residential construction industry to communicate with consumers this way. If potential buyers are not talking to or about you, it's time for you to use blogs and social media to kick-start the conversation.

Carol Flammer, outlines in a clear, concise, no-nonsense style just how to go about engaging these consumers. This book speaks specifically to the needs of the real estate industry, and home builders in particular, in building a social media presence.

Social Media for Home Builders will show you how to incorporate this growing medium in practical ways that will help your business grow. Let this book guide you to engage today's new home customers.

–Paul Chaney, author, *The Digital Handshake*

Preface

As early as 2005, an IRM/Harris Interactive[1] study found that the overwhelming majority of new home shoppers start their home search online. Builders were surprised by this finding. Their marketing channels still emphasized traditional media and strategies. With 90% of buyers now shopping online for new homes and communities, builders must understand how and where to make their homes visible on the web.

I have been immersed in social media since 2005 (or "new media" as it was called way back then). My colleagues and I tested the waters by posting press releases to a mixture of paid and free online distribution services and pitching stories to real estate agents' blogs. Then one day it occurred to me that I could easily populate a market-focused blog with stories from our clients. With that, Atlanta Real Estate Forum was born into an industry that was skeptical of anything online beyond a basic website.

Now, six years later, Atlanta Real Estate Forum is not only a nationally ranked blog; it's the largest real-estate-focused blog in Atlanta. The site reaches more than 20,000 unique visitors a month. Forty percent of its traffic comes from outside of Georgia. More importantly, the blog sends 200–450 traffic units or more per month to home builders who participate and post content on it. But electronic media barely takes a breath before moving on to the next big thing. Some say that with the proliferation of social networking sites, blogging has become passé.

However, success with social media—like any public relations (PR) or marketing strategy—is not about jumping from one "latest thing" to another. You build a winning strategy by carefully choosing and targeting audiences. You must use resources wisely. These resources include your time, which can be completely consumed by social media without smart strategies for managing online networking. Personalized communication and give-and-take, rather than mass media messaging and selling, govern the social media universe. You must give something back, even if it's just honest conversation. If you are a green builder, for example, in addition to promoting your green homes online, you can offer tips for the average consumer who wants to live a greener lifestyle.

As a home builder engaged in social media, you will strategically place "directional signs" on the Internet to help home seekers find you. You will also build online relationships with people and companies who influence consumers throughout their buying process. As Paul Chaney says in *The Digital Handshake*,[2] "Social Media is much more than a toolset, it is a mind-set as well."

The newest form of permission-based marketing, social media marketing, is ever changing and evolving. On the surface, much social networking dialog may seem like idle chatter, but so does cocktail-party conversation or the back-and-forth over 18 holes on the golf course. An important difference between these traditional networking activities and social media marketing, however, is that you can use the latter opportunity to build brand, engage consumers, manage your online reputation, and sell homes—virally and exponentially. To do these things successfully, however, you need the right tools and a comprehensive marketing strategy. Social media can be "easier than you think" when you build from a proper foundation. Make the investment to launch a program with clear goals, messaging, and, most importantly, properly built websites and social sites.

This book will help you create a long-term marketing strategy for building and maintaining an effective social media presence. Happy reading! I hope to connect with you online soon.

http://www.Facebook.com/carolflammer
http://www.Linkedin.com/in/carolflammer
http://Twitter.com/carolflammer
http://www.CarolFlammer.com
http://www.mRELEVANCE.com

Acknowledgments

I extend a heartfelt thanks to my husband and the rest of my family, who look past the craziness of my ideas to see possibilities. Also, to the team members at Flammer Relations and mRELEVANCE: I owe you a debt of gratitude for the hard work and dedication that transform many of those ideas into reality. To my business partner Mitch Levinson, who was willing to weave his areas of expertise with mine to create great outcomes for our families, our businesses, and our industry: Thank you. I also want to give special thanks to my brother, David Morgan, who built my first blog, http://www.Atlanta RealEstateForum.com, taught me about search engine optimization, and opened a world of opportunity. Finally, special thanks to all of my friends and clients who have supported and inspired me along the way.

The Growth of Social Media

Celebrities are tweeting, newspapers are blogging, and often the only way you can "talk" to your children or grandchildren is on their Facebook walls. But what does all of this electronic chatter have to do with selling a home? Online networking, blogging, and tweeting have changed the buying process (fig. 1.1): search engines, websites, and *blogs* are leading the way for businesses to promote and consumers to find and purchase big-ticket items costing $25,000 or more.[3]

An unpublished survey by *Big Builder* magazine[4] of industry professionals found similar results to other national surveys of how businesses are integrating on-line tools into their marketing strategies. The findings demonstrated that social media marketing through sites such as Ning, Twitter, Facebook, and others can help you refine your strategy, increase your reach, and measure your effectiveness better than traditional print advertising. With reduced marketing budgets, many

Figure 1.1 Internet purchasing habits

Many tried-and-true marketing methods have been replaced by methods with more consumer engagement, such as social marketing.

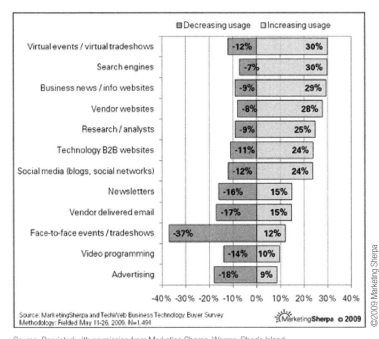

Source: Reprinted with permission from Marketing Sherpa, Warren, Rhode Island

companies, including home builders, have turned to *social media* to bridge the gap between their product and their potential customers, as the following responses demonstrate:

Social media is the array of Internet tools that enables interaction and conversations among users. Among other tools, these include blogs, *wikis*, forums, videos, *social bookmarking*, and *social networking* sites. Unlike early websites, which were static like a brochure, social media sites are interactive and encourage users to converse, opine, and lend expertise. They urge users to add original content.

- 60% said they were active in the social media sphere.
- 34% said they were considering becoming active.
- 85% of builder respondents used Facebook and Twitter the most of all the social networking sites.
- 80% used Linkedin.
- 45% used blogs.
- 37% used craigslist.
- 83% of respondents said their primary reason for social networking was to increase brand recognition.
- 67% were using social networking to drive traffic and sales.

- 67% were using social networking to generate sales leads.

Participants in a recent National Association of Home Builders (NAHB) Professional Women in Building webinar[5] were asked in an online poll "What types of social media are you using for your business?" The results were as follows:

- Facebook—73%
- Linkedin—51%
- YouTube—24%
- Blogs—22%
- Twitter—19%
- Other—14%

The striking difference between the percentage of respondents who were using Facebook and those who had blogs indicates that 78% are not managing their online presence as efficiently as they could be. A well-built blog should be the engine of your entire social media program. It integrates your program and reduces the work required to manage all of your online sites. By creating a blog first, companies can reduce the time requirement for managing social media by 50%. Moreover, blogging combined with social networking has helped builders increase traffic to their websites by 25%–50%. It's not surprising, then, that market research predicts 43% of businesses will be blogging by 2012.[6]

Real Results from Social Media

Builders who have embraced social media strategically have achieved the following results:

- 25%–300% increase in website traffic
- 200 new Realtor connections
- Article in a major newspaper
- Referrals from friends
- Coupons redeemed for new home purchases

Your social media program could have similar outcomes.

Builders and others in the home building industry have embraced blogging and created an extensive presence or brand through social media as follows:

Acadia Homes and Neighborhoods blog (http://www.AcadiaHomes.us) integrates seamlessly into the Acadia Homes website as its news section.

Greater Valley Group Real Estate (http://www.GVG RealEstate.com) uses its blog to share news about its communities, apartments, hotels, and available commercial property. The site links to various company websites. The blog is a search magnet: 75% of its traffic is new visitors.

The S&A Homes blog (http://www.SAHomesBlog.com) quickly became a top referral source for the company's main website. Within the first 30 days of launch, well over 900 people visited the blog and more than 60% of them were new visitors. S&A Homes builds in Pennsylvania and West Virginia. The company has 45 active communities.

Boone Homes blog (http://www.BooneHomesBlog.com) provides the home builder with more ways to share messages with its audiences. The blog is the builder's number one website referral source, sending traffic that visits more than eight pages and spends more than six minutes on the site.

Traton Homes blog (http://www.TratonHomesBlog.com) is a top referral source to the home builder's main website. The blog makes it easy to find all of the builder's social media sites with prominently placed social media buttons. There is also a prominent link to "Visit Our website" that ensures traffic ultimately finds the builder's site.

Construction Resources blog (http://www.ConstructionResourcesBlog.com) showcases the latest products, sales, and events. This supplier uses the blog to tie all of its online activity together and increase traffic to its main website.

Who Uses Social Media?

Social media platforms have received broad acceptance across all demographic groups, including baby boomers, women, Gen X, and of course, Gen Y.

Baby Boomers

According to the Pew Research Center,[7] the number of baby boomers past age 50 who use social networking nearly doubled in one year–from 22% to 42%. Although they still communicate primarily through e-mail with friends, family, and business contacts, most now use social networking platforms to help manage their daily communications.

Boomers are using Facebook to keep up with their children's and grandchildren's activities. Social media helps geographically dispersed families breach long distances and facilitates working parents communicating with their children. My mother, like my friends, is just as likely to contact me through Facebook mail or a wall post as she is to pick up the phone and call me. Additionally, boomers use social sites to stay involved with the groups they belong to in real life (*IRL*). From the church choir to their local animal shelter, boomers are using social media to maintain meaningful networks of communities.

From April 2009 to May 2010, social networking among Internet users ages 50–64 grew by 88%–from 25% to 47%.

During the same period, use by those 65 and older doubled from 13% to 26%.

Social networking use among Internet users ages 18–29 grew by 13%, from 76% to 86%.

Women

Women have embraced social media for networking and opinion sharing even more than the general population. Social networking provides a conduit to reach old friends and make new acquaintances. A 2010 study by comScore[8] concluded that women are the digital mainstream. They are highly engaged online if you know where to look for them.

Besides being online shoppers, women are attracted to community and lifestyle sites, especially those with parenting, food, and home-related content. Although sports, automotive, and online trading sites are still strongholds for men, women are just as likely as men to manage money online.

Moreover, social networking is central to women's Internet experience. They embrace social networking differently than men.

- Females older than 15 spend 8% more time online than males.
- More than half (56%) of adult women use the Internet to connect with people, compared with 46% of adult men.
- Women spent an average of 16.3% of their online time on social networks in April 2010, compared with 11.7% among men online.

Social networking's reach is highest among women in North America, with 9 out of 10 female Internet users visiting a social networking site in April 2010.

Of women who participated in any social media activity weekly or more (about half of the sample used social media daily), 75% participated in social networks.[9] They used social media platforms such as Facebook to communicate with friends and family and to share family photos, plan outings with "the girls," and just "talk." Fifty-five percent blogged and 20% used Twitter. The women reported spending less time following mass media, including television, newspapers, magazines, and radio, than previously.

The Chief Marketer[10] reported that men use social media sites to find information (36% versus 28% of women) and women use the sites to find coupons and promotions to stretch their budgets (47% versus 33% of men).

Gen Y

Dan Schawbel, author of *Me 2.0: Build a Powerful Brand to Achieve Career Success* and owner of Mashable, an online guide to social media, says "Gen Y was raised on technology. They have always had e-mail and the ability to text. Their cell phones are extensions of their hands. They use them to text message, instant message (IM), and check their Facebook page. There are many different ways to interact with GenY, but you'll find most of them are already on Facebook."[11]

However, social media not is a one-stop solution for reaching GenY. So-called *refuseniks* that are also part of this generation choose to remain off the social networking grid. These age 20-to-early-30s Gen Y-ers prefer privacy and face-to-face communications. Generally, they have less education and disposable income than their peers who have chosen to embrace social media. In fact, social networkers in general are more likely than nonusers to have annual incomes of $75,000 or more. The latter group is more likely to have only a high school education.[12]

The fastest growing age group on Twitter is youths and young adults (ages 12–24).

Where Consumers Are

With so many choices of social networking sites, how do you know where to focus your efforts? Four sites you don't want to overlook when creating your social media marketing program are Facebook, YouTube, Twitter, and your self-hosted blog.

Facebook

With more than 400 million users,[13] Facebook is now the world's fourth largest "continent"! Fifty percent of active Facebook users log on daily. People 35 and older are the fastest growing demographic on Facebook.

- The average user has 130 friends on the site.
- The average user is connected to 80 pages, groups, and events.
- More than 60 million status updates are posted each day.
- More than 30 million users become *fans* of pages each day.
- 200 million active users access Facebook through their mobile devices.
- People who use mobile devices to access the site are twice as active on it.

Facebook's growth in the U.S. is staggering. IStrategy Labs[14] tracked the growth of the popular site from 2009 to 2010. Here are the findings:

- Facebook's US user base grew from 42 million to 103 million (144.9%) in 2009.
- People 35 and older are now more than 30% of the entire user base.
- The 55+ audience grew 922.7% in 2009.
- Atlanta had the highest growth rate among US cities in 2009 at 267.6%

YouTube

YouTube[15] has global reach. Its users generally are 18–55 and evenly distributed between males and females.

- 51% of users visit YouTube at least weekly.
- 51% of 18–34-year-olds often share YouTube videos with friends and colleagues.
- Two billion videos a day are viewed on YouTube.
- Hundreds of thousands of videos are uploaded to You Tube daily. In fact, every minute, 24 hours of video is uploaded to YouTube.

Twitter

Twitter has more than 100 million registered users, with some 300,000 new users registering each day.[16] Every month, 180 million unique visitors go to the site. Here's what they do:

- 37% of active Twitter users tweet from their phone.
- 75% of Twitter traffic accesses the site via third party *applications*.

Tweets total an average of 55 million daily. Twitter's search engine receives some 600 million search queries per day.

Your Self-Hosted Blog

Technorati, the world's largest blog directory, indexes more than 1.25 million blogs worldwide. Technorati's State of the Blogosphere 2010[17] shows that 49% of bloggers worldwide are based in the United States. Only 1% are corporate bloggers; 21% of US bloggers are self-employed. But corporate bloggers receive the most unique visitors a month. You can attract new visitors to your site by blogging. Blogging is an excellent way to increase your Internet traffic, increase visitors coming from referring sites, and increase *search engine optimization* through the expansion of *keywords*.

Making Social Media Work for You

Your social media toolbox includes these five elements:

1. Company website (which may be a blog)
2. Blog
3. Online Public Relations (PR)
4. Social networking sites
5. Other sites

To effectively apply these tools, you must first understand three key components of a social media strategy: marketing, networking, and optimization.

Social media marketing (SMM) is the strategic creation and distribution of content and messages throughout the Internet via social media, social networking (Linkedin, Facebook), and social bookmarking. SMM encompasses almost every interaction you have online. As with other marketing efforts, you must carefully plan these interactions and deliver them to targeted audiences to achieve a goal.

Social media optimization (SMO) is using social media outlets to boost a website's ranking in search engines, such as Google. This powerful tool increases traffic on your website by expanding the number of keywords and referring URLs search engines will find. Keywords are words or phrases that will direct an Internet user to a relevant web page. For example, searching for "Chicago green home builders" will return links to websites that are most relevant for these keywords. Social media optimization also refers to the process of optimizing each individual social network for the search engines. This involves getting *custom* or *vanity URLs* for the sites and ensuring that each site properly links to all of the other sites in your program.

Social networking is all about engaging others by creating online communities where you and others interact and converse. Facebook, Linkedin, Twitter and ActiveRain are among the social networking sites that allow you to have conversations and create relationships with friends, fans, and followers. When you understand how SMM can help improve your company's visibility and increase traffic on your website, you can formulate a strategy to maximize its impact.

Social Media Marketing Strategy

No self-respecting home builder would break ground on a new home without having a plan. Likewise, no social media program should move forward without a blueprint for success. Whether a plan strives to meet one goal or five, it must define what is most important to your social media marketing program. Setting goals allows you to create a sound strategy now and measure *return on investment* (*ROI*) later. Goals must be specific and measurable. Strategies are the steps you will take to meet those goals.

Social Media Marketing Goals

- Increased website traffic
- SMO
- Reputation management
- Engagement through social networking
- Building brand

Increasing Website Traffic

Participating in social media and social networking can help you increase the traffic to your main website and your blog. More traffic equals more buyers. Post relevant content online on blogs, social networking sites, and through online public relations, incorporating links to the primary website and your blog. This will increase the number of referring URLs for these sites. Links provide Internet shoppers more opportunities to click and connect to your website and find your business online. Think of it as weaving a bigger web or placing more directional signs to a model home in all the right places. Appearing in all the places where consumers are already online (like the social networking sites) is like using a big funnel: You capture many users' attention and then focus their search so they eventually land on your website. Leading more traffic to your website can increase the number of lead conversions because effective social media programs tend to garner more qualified leads. Sterling Custom Homes demonstrates the effects of a strong *search engine optimization* (*SEO*) and SMO program through increased traffic year-over-year (fig. 2.1).

SEO uses specific strategies to boost your website's ranking in search results for a variety of keywords or phrases. Both on-page (on the website) and off-page (e.g., links, articles, other sites) can achieve positive *organic results*. Organic results appear because of their *relevance* to the term being searched. They are not paid advertisements or *pay-per-click* results. The term *search engine marketing* typically refers to marketing via both paid and organic search. If you are purchasing this ser-

Figure 2.1 Sterling Custom Homes website traffic

Tracking website traffic year-over-year allows businesses to gauge improvement in traffic from one year to the next. It also identifies seasonal traffic trends that allow for more effective marketing strategy and budgeting.

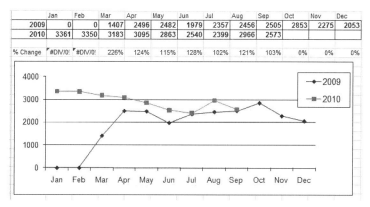

	Jan	Feb	Mar	Apr	May	Jun	Jul	Aug	Sep	Oct	Nov	Dec
2009	0	0	1407	2496	2482	1979	2357	2456	2505	2853	2275	2053
2010	3361	3350	3183	3095	2863	2540	2399	2966	2573			
% Change	#DIV/0!	#DIV/0!	226%	124%	115%	128%	102%	121%	103%	0%	0%	0%

Source: Reprinted with Permission from Sterling Custom Homes Inc., Austin, Texas

vice, ask what you are actually buying because often companies selling a search engine marketing service will call it search engine optimization.

SMO (SEO's Cousin)

With 85% of shoppers using Google, Yahoo!, Bing, or another search engine to start their online searches, a sound SMO plan should first identify the search terms buyers use to find you or companies like yours online. Next, integrate these search terms as keywords into your blog posts, *online public relations (PR)*, and the other content you post as part of your social media marketing program. When these keywords are used as *anchor text*, search engines will identify your site as relevant for these words and phrases.

To maximize returns from using the Internet, you must think like a search engine. This is especially important when blogging and posting to social media sites. One source of information about how Internet shoppers are finding your website currently is your *analytics* account. Therefore, you should have an analytics account for both your website and your blog. Many companies use Google Analytics, which provides data for free, but many other programs are available–both free and fee based. Among these are Yahoo!, Webtrends, AWStats, and Urchin.

Anchor text is the underlined word or phrase a user sees and can click to activate a *hyperlink* to another web page. Search engines rank anchor text highly in determining the subject and relevance of a page. Anchor text is sometimes referred to as "linked text."

Reputation Management

When you Google your name, do you like what you see? More importantly, when your prospective buyers Google your name, do *they* like what they see?

If you don't like your *search engine results page (SERP)*, you should implement an SMM campaign ASAP! If you find an unhappy customer's blogs or negative sites on page one of your company's results, you can be certain that potential customers will find them too. To manage your reputation, fill your page-one SERPs with desirable results. A well-built blog and a website with proper SEO should appear consistently among the first four results for your name. You can easily fill up the rest of your page-one results with posts to online PR and social networking sites such as Facebook, ActiveRain, Trulia®, Twitter, YouTube, and Flickr®—to name just a few favorites.

The specific negative results you have for your name and the strength of those sites will determine how quickly they can be minimized and "moved" to page two. Strong SMO and SEO programs contribute greatly to minimizing the position and impact of negative information.

Gerstad Builders demonstrates textbook page one SERP results (fig. 2.2). The sites that browsers see when they Google "Gerstad Builders" include those the builder created (main website and blog), social networks the company participates in, external blogs where company representatives post, online PR articles, and media coverage of the company. Whether they visit Twitter, YouTube, or Facebook, consumers will find easy ways to access the builder's website.

Figure 2.2 Gerstad Builders SERP results

Make sure to search your company's name from time to time. Identify the search results you want on page one and create a plan to meet your goals over time.

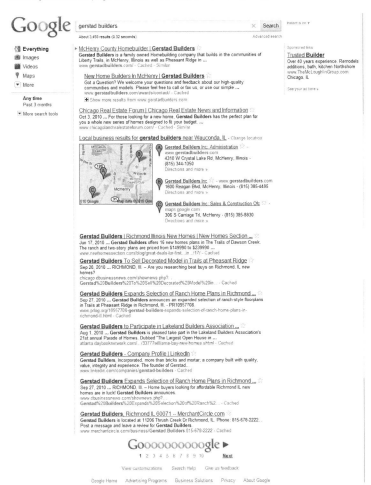

Source: Reprinted with permission from Gerstad Builders, McHenry, Illinois

mRELEVANCE's launch of the Gerstad Builders SMM campaign in early 2010 completely changed the results of Internet browsing for the company. Instead of irrelevant or random websites, Internet searchers now get the "yellow pages" of all the places to find and interact with Gerstad Builders online:

- Company blog and website
- Articles on Green Built Blog
- Articles on Chicagoland Real Estate Forum
- Linkedin profile
- Online press releases

The engine of Gerstad Builders' program is a highly optimized website built on a blog platform. Other components of the program such as Twitter, Facebook, and ancillary blogs are places for home buyers and Realtors to interact with the builder and find out about current promotions and incentives. Blog posts keep web references about the builder fresh and increase traffic to its website. The referral traffic to Gerstad Builders' website has quadrupled since the company launched its new blog/website.

Engagement Through Social Networking

The most popular social networks today are Facebook, Linkedin, Twitter, and YouTube. But just being visible on these networks will not build your brand or increase your qualified lead traffic. Unlike push media such as print or radio advertising, social networking is about starting and engaging in conversations, interacting with others, and forming relationships. Customers and potential customers want to understand you and discover your company's personality and culture.

Your social networking should fulfill your brand promise and positioning. If you promote that you are a customer-service-oriented company, your customers might just test you. Launching pages on Twitter and Facebook tells your customers that you are ready and willing to converse with them, so think twice before jumping on social networking sites to merely blast your latest offer out to the masses. Actually talking with your customers and potential customers creates the top-of-mind awareness that starts to build online brand. Your first conversations will provide an early indicator of whether you will be successful.

Consumers who embrace social media want to know what's in it for them. The main reason consumers friend, fan, or follow brands is to get something. It's all about the "me" in social media. As a business, you must provide social networkers with a reason to follow you, such as a coupon or incentive just for the fans that *Like* you on Facebook, or information that educates them or helps them solve a problem.

Define your audience for each social network. Having thousands of friends, fans, and followers is only effective if they are the right ones. Who do you want to reach and what is the right network for each target audience? Consider the following groups:

- Current customers and clients (homeowners)
- Future customers and clients (active home seekers)
- *Influencers* (industry professionals, government officials, and cheerleaders who may not be related to your company but who will share your messages)

Building Brand

Companies large and small, including competitors that you may or may not be aware of, are building brand online every minute. Online branding is a comparatively inexpensive marketing alternative ideal for financially challenging times. A first step in branding your company online is ensuring that your company logo and colors are on every website you participate in. This is your chance to extend your brand beyond your own website and printed materials. You will avoid confusing consumers if you have a clear brand and messaging. Brand goes beyond your logo and promises made in a print ad: it is a lasting impression of your company that can begin with how you and your team answer the phones, how you sign your e-mail messages, and what Internet users find when they search your name online.

Online consumers also learn about you by where they don't find you. When they Google your name, can prospects find you? Do you appear at the top of SERP results when they Google your *unique selling proposition (USP)*? (Yes, USPs apply to online as well as traditional marketing.) Or are they finding your main competitor first? Prospective buyers must be able to locate you where they think you should be, not only in the search engines, but also on social media sites. Can they find and engage with you on Twitter, Facebook, Ning, forums, and your blog?

Set Goals

The adage that you can't get where you are going if you *don't* know where you want to end up certainly applies to social media marketing. You must create a plan, measure results, and focus on milestones. Whether you want to build brand or manage your reputation, milestones could include launching a blog, optimizing the blog to be among your top five referral sources, or getting 200 Realtor fans on Facebook.

Create Your Strategy

By putting social media tools to work in building SMM and SMO plans, you will attract more online buyers, build a stronger brand, create more loyal customers, and ultimately, increase sales. Although marketing today is different than it was before the Internet, you don't have to reinvent everything. Think about how to adapt what you are doing now to today's marketing environment. You should incorporate SMM into an overall marketing plan just as you do Internet marketing, SEO, agent events, advertising, and PR. You can use stories, messages, and events to encourage conversations and spontaneity. However, a sound social media strategy ends, rather than begins, with social networking sites. Before you can have SMO, you must first optimize your website and blog.

Integrating social media into your overall marketing mix will streamline your program and make it more effective. Think of your blog or your blog/website as the engine of your program. Your *editorial calendar* will revolve around your blog and the blog will pull the entire marketing program together.

Your company's blog or your blog/website links all of your sites together and drives your online image (fig. 2.3). It is like the hub of a wheel and the engine of a car. No matter what other sites come and go, if you

Figure 2.3 The social marketing web

A sound marketing strategy includes social networking, social bookmarking, and photo sharing sites; search engines; syndication (RSS feeds); and e-mail marketing. All roads lead back to your website and blog.

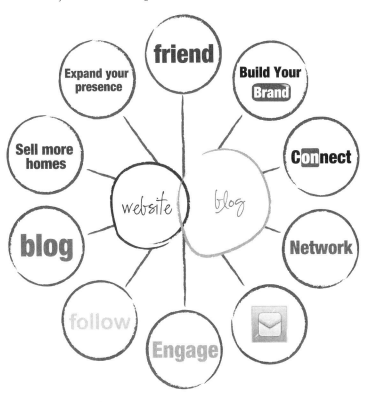

Source: mRELEVANCE, LLC

have built your program around the piece that you own (your blog or website), you will still have a strong online presence that can go the distance. Because your blog is the engine of your program, you won't have to worry about what sites are hot today that might become "not" tomorrow. Your blog becomes your content machine: use it to build your program and as the popularity of third-party sites comes and goes, your blog will remain "in fashion."

Websites and Blogs

Your website is central to ensuring the effectiveness of all of your other online communication. Whether your site is a traditional one or a blog, its elements should build on one another. Construct your site with proper keywords, title *tags*, metadata, and SEO before launching a social media program. The website (or blog) should be

- *sticky* (able to hold users' attention and encourage them to visit multiple pages on the site);
- built with *web 2.0* in mind (interactive so browsers can participate in it and engage with you);
- programmed to capture leads by including multiple ways for Internet shoppers to provide their names and e-mail addresses; and
- easily navigated using mobile devices.

Connected Consumers

Smartphone sales outpaced personal computer sales in 2010. Smartphone manufacturers shipped 100.9 million devices in fourth quarter 2010 compared with 92.1 million personal computers.[18] Moreover, the Pew Internet and American Life project[19] says 90% of Americans own a computerized gadget, such as a cell phone, computer, MP3 player, game console, e-book reader, or tablet computer. Smartphones and handheld devices are abundant. Make sure users can navigate your site with these devices.

- 93% of U.S. adults own a cell phone.
- 23% of Americans access the web from mobile devices each day.
- Google has a separate index for mobile content.

Mitch Levinson,[20] MIRM, CSP, managing partner with mRELEVANCE, says that an effective website is

- attractive;
- search-engine friendly;
- interactive;
- effective at capturing contact information;
- easy to navigate;
- consistent with the company's brand and capabilities; and
- focused on the target market.

When consumers land on your website from social media sites, they form an impression of your company that can prompt them to either keep your company on their list or cross you off, he says. It must be compelling in order to be effective.

Website Musts

An effective website will have the following 10 attributes:

1. **Proper SEO.** A website with proper SEO is built in a search-engine-friendly language and contains appropriate keywords and relevant title tags. For example, a custom home builder in Des Moines, Iowa might incorporate the following keywords: Des Moines custom homes, Des Moines custom builder, and custom homes in Des Moines. The main title tag on its home page might read: Name of Building Company–Des Moines Iowa Custom Homes–Luxury Custom Home Builder.

2. **Appropriate keywords.** These relevant words define your business. Also consider the search volume for these words. If people do not know the name of your company, how will they find you? You can use keywords to help them! In the previous example, the descriptors "Des Moines custom homes," "Des Moines custom builder," and "custom homes in Des

Moines" can help search engines to locate you. If you focus on energy-efficient green homes or specific areas or communities, you will want to add descriptors appropriate for those areas. We usually start by brainstorming with the entire team, which includes everyone who works with the home builder or remodeler. We develop a long list of words and then narrow it down by reviewing search statistics for the quantity and volume of search performed for each word. We also assess the competition for that word, using Google Insights for Search.

3. **Relevant title tags.** These appropriate keywords are search-engine targeted and appear at the top of a website. Each page should have a unique title tag. Too often, builders have home pages titled "Home Page." Be sure to label each page of your website with relevant keywords. For example, an interior web page might be labeled: Name of Building Company–Homes Under Construction–Warren County Home Builder.

4. **Appealing visuals.** Pictures not only must be eye-catching and appealing, but also user-friendly. Think about the home plans you've seen online that are of poor quality, too small, or otherwise difficult to read. Use professional photography and make sure your homes are in pristine condition, including finished landscaping. Note the composition of your

photos; anything that detracts from your homes' appearance must be removed, including dumpsters, temporary power poles, temporary yard signage, rock piles, and portable toilets.

5. **Honest representation of company.** Credible information is not only factual but also relevant to the products the company builds. If you build entry-level homes in Atlanta, optimize your site for first-time buyers and avoid words like "luxury," which might attract a higher-income repeat buyer. The latter buyers will leave your site because your homes are not what they are looking for.

6. **Lead capture.** You must drive website visitors to a contact form to complete so you can capture their information and create a lead. One popular way to do this is with landing pages tailored to specific users. For example, when a potential buyer clicks to your page from Twitter, offer them an incentive on a landing page you have built just for visitors from Twitter. The incentive could be entry into a quarterly drawing for a $25 gift card or some other reward.

7. **Easy navigation.** Your site must be intuitive. Users must be able to find what they are looking for quickly and easily. Ensure they can find your plans and pricing within two to three clicks. Organized navigation is key! Make sure you don't have so

much navigation that visitors cannot find any-thing. Can they find what they are looking for in two to three clicks? Enlist volunteers within and outside of your company. Give them a list of items to find on your website (e.g., home prices, avail-able floorplans, contact information) and ask them to note how many clicks it takes them to find the information.

8. **Stickiness.** A sticky website holds a user's atten-tion, measured by the amount of time he or she spends on it and how deeply the visitor delves into it. You want visitors to spend three to eight minutes on your site viewing multiple pages. You can track progress toward this benchmark over time using Google Analytics or programs like it. Note the web pages where users spend the most time, which land-ing pages pop up most frequently, and which pages users are on when they exit your site. You can see which pages are the most popular and interesting, and which ones might need fresh content.

9. **Social media interconnectivity.** Make sure your site gives browsers a way to find all of your social media sites including your blog, Facebook page, LinkedIn profile, and Twitter feed. Often the infor-mation and connections buyers make through so-cial media convert online visitors into buyers.

10. **Call to action.** The website must guide the user to interact with you. It should seek user contact information and provide various options for a user to contact you. Use the website to encourage visitors to call the telephone number on your site, drive to your sales center, or contact you via your online contact form. Provide multiple ways for people to contact you by including all of your community phone numbers on the site, contact forms for each community, and a form that users can complete to start receiving your newsletter.

The Blog as a Website

Glen Lake, an Atlanta apartment community, uses a blog for its main website (fig. 3.1). Savvy Web development teams are building sites using *content management systems (CMS)* that were created specifically for blogging. If you are building a new website and want it to contain a blog, use these systems. Like printed brochures, most websites are designed to be updated less frequently than a blog. However, content management software with a user interface, such as WordPress, facilitates frequent updates. In addition to blogging, nontechnical users can learn to update other areas of the site using content management software.

Figure 3.1 Glen Lake's blog/website home page

Your custom blog can look just like a website. In fact, it can be your website!

Source: Reprinted with permission from Jason Schlesinger, Stamford, Connecticut

Why Blog?

A properly built blog is the engine that drives a successful social media program. When you combine great writing, phenomenal images, and SMO in a blog, you have a formula for success. Companies should blog for three primary reasons: (1) to better control the company's image and reputation, (2) to increase the search engine optimization of the main website (through SMO), and (3) to create a platform to engage and interact with buyers.

Besides engaging online shoppers in an informal conversation, a well-built blog can expand the SEO of the main website by increasing the number of keywords and referring URLs—two objectives of social media optimization.

Proven Success

Industry-focused blogs such as Atlanta Real Estate Green Built Blog (http://www.GreenBuiltBlog.com) demonstrate the value of blogs (fig. 3.2). They provide a space for multiple companies to attract potential buyers through the search engines. Sites like this help builders expand their keyword reach through SMO. With hundreds of keywords indexed by Google per month, this site is a top referral source for many Atlanta home builders, developers, and their communities.

Figure 3.2 Green Built Blog

A highly optimized new homes news blog featuring green building news, Green Built Blog attracts about 45% of its traffic from consumers searching keywords in the search engines.

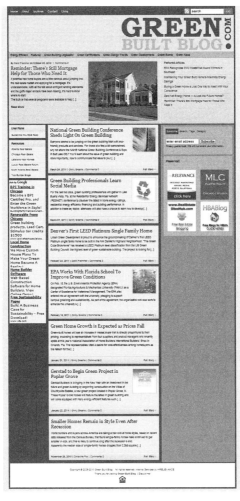

The blog connects buyers to a company website through search. Although most websites can be optimized for only 5–10 keywords, a blog can attract search engines with hundreds or even thousands of keywords. By expanding keywords and anchor text, blogging can increase the traffic to a website exponentially. By design, when a new post is written and published, a new page is created on the blog. Fresh content keeps attracting the search engines and providing new pages to index. Your website's relevance vis-à-vis keywords in the posts continually increases. Your blog can grow by as many as eight pages a month (if you add eight posts a month), whereas most websites don't add new pages monthly, even if the sites are updated. This is one of the main reasons that a well-built blog will perform well with the search engines over time.

Of all the tools, sites, and social media strategies, a blog is the one likeliest to net ROI and show almost instant success. A well-built, optimized blog will become a top referral source for the company website. Your blog will probably be among your top five website referral sources within a few weeks of launching it.

What's in a Blog?

The word blog is a contraction of two words, Web and log. A type of website, originally blogs were like online diaries or journals.

Today the blog is a site focused on a particular subject or area of expertise. Posts are displayed in reverse chronological order: the most recent post will display at the top of the page.

Blog software is open source and is frequently updated. To maintain a blog's functionality, keep *plug-ins* working, and reduce security risks, blog software must be updated as new versions are released. Depending on the complexity of your WordPress site, up-dating your software can be as easy as clicking a link to update it.

Establish the objectives for your blog, such as

- attracting search engines;
- enticing readers to visit the company's main website;
- encouraging direct company contact and interaction; and
- building participation in an online or offline event or activity.

Traton Homes Attracts Traffic

Traton Homes embraced social media with the launch of http://www.TratonHomesBlog.com (fig. 3.3). Traton Homes is a Marietta, Georgia, builder of townhomes and single family homes throughout the Atlanta metro area.

The blog offers prospective home buyers the op-portunity to connect with the company and learn more about Traton's homes, communities, and the company. It increases keywords and referring URLs for the com-pany's main website.

Figure 3.3 Traton Homes blog

The Traton Homes blog is a top referral source for the Traton Homes website.

Source: Reprinted with permission from Traton Homes, Marietta, Georgia.

Within 30 days of launch, the blog became one of the top 10 referral sources for the company's main website. More than 50% of traffic to the company's blog was from search engines and free referral sources. Overall, more than 70% of traffic to the blog is new traffic. If you Google "Traton Homes," page one search results will include Atlanta Real Estate Forum, the company's Twitter feed link, several other blogs the company participates in, and online PR stories.

The Traton Homes blog keeps home buyers abreast of community news, local events, and special promotions. The blog also features videos of specific communities and the home page always features a community. Home shoppers will enjoy being able to access the builder's top selling communities directly from the blog.

Creating Your Blog: Getting Started with WordPress

Follow these 12 steps to create a self-hosted WordPress blog and measure its effectiveness:

1. **Name your blog.** http://www.NameofCompanyBlog. com is a popular choice. Another option many companies choose is http://www.NameofCompany News.com. You can purchase your domain name from a domain reseller like http://www.GoDaddy. com, http://www.Register.com, or http://www. Domain.com.

2. **Determine hosting for your blog.** Your blog can be hosted on the same server as your main website, but often you will need to explore other options. Some low-cost options include http://www.BlueHost.com and http://www.HostGator.com, but consider in-

stead hosting your site at a premium hosting location. This will provide you with more control so that no known *spammers* are hosted with you. You will also be able to get a unique ISP address for your site.

3. **Choose a *theme* and categories.** Many free or inexpensive templates and themes are available for blogs, or a web developer can create a custom theme for you. You can choose from a number of free themes at WordPress.org.[21]

4. **Determine keywords.** What words will customers use to find you? Make sure you have a plan for using them in your blog. For example if you build energy-efficient homes, you will want to include "energy efficient homes" in your list of keywords along with "<u>Name of City</u> real estate," "_____ sized lots in <u>Name of City</u>," and other variations.

5. **Go to http://www.wordpress.org to download blogging software to your URL.** You will want to research available themes and plug-ins and download those as well. Most people will need to hire a web developer to complete this step.

6. **Create an editorial calendar.** Set a schedule for posting on your blog. You should publish eight entries per month. Vary the days you post to keep the search engines guessing about when you will post. Internet traffic is highest during the week, so post Monday through Friday.

7. **Create a blog policy.** It should address how comments will be moderated. Following is a sample blog policy. (Refer to Resources or Google "blog policy" for other examples.)

Atlanta Real Estate Forum Blog Policy

Disclosures

In order to comply with recent FTC Rulings, Atlanta Real Estate Forum discloses the following: This blog was launched as an online extension of public relations coverage for Flammer Relation's and mRELEVANCE's clients. The site accepts advertisements and currently has more than 100 contributors from the Atlanta real estate industry. The blog also covers industry news via our team of talented reporters. Non-profit news is covered as a community service. Oh, and yes, those are Google ads on the left side of the site.

Rules of Engagement

By posting to Atlanta Real Estate Forum you agree that you are responsible for the content you contribute, link to, or otherwise upload. All posts and comments must be related to the subject matter covered by this site (real estate). You agree not to post anything threatening, libelous, defamatory, obscene, inflammatory, illegal or pornographic, or anything that infringes upon the copyright, trademark, publicity rights or other rights of a third party.

We welcome comments, but please understand that all comments are moderated and reviewed for relevance to site topics. Comments and posts will be published at the sole discretion of mRELEVANCE. Your valid e-mail address must be used when you post or comment. It will not be published, but may be used to confirm your identity or contact you with questions.

Atlanta Real Estate Forum strives for accuracy; however, with the large number of contributors on the site we assume no liability for errors or omissions. You transfer rights to Atlanta Real Estate Forum for any original content you provide.

By using our Site, you agree to our policies and rules of engagement.

8. **Assemble your blogging team.** This is not necessarily your marketing team. Which staff members love to write or shoot video? Include them! We work with a number of blogging teams that include

members of the sales team, design center representatives, and the president or CEO of the home
building company.

9. **Launch your site.** Change the *A record* or name
servers in your DNS (domain name server) account
to point to the new blog and make it live. It can take
up to 24 hours to propagate through the Internet.

10. **Install Google Analytics.** You can find a step-by-
step guide for adding this *tracking* software to your
blog at Google (http://www.google.com/support/
analytics/bin/answer.py?hl=en&answer=66983).

11. **Promote your blog.** Burn the *really simple syndication (RSS)* feed, and connect the blog to Twitter,
Facebook, and other social networking sites. Register the blog on blog catalogs such as Technorati,
Blog Catalog, and Best of the Web.

12. **Measure results.** Use Google Analytics to track key
performance indicators such as number of visitors,
time on site, and most popular content.

Free Blogging Options

Free blogging options include the complimentary version of WordPress (http://www.wordpress.com), Blogger (http://www.blogger.com), or Real Estate Sites Hub
(http://www.RealEstateSitesHub.com).

You also can blog on industry sites such as Active-Rain, Trulia, RealtyJoin, or Realtor.com, and on local blogs where you can share your expertise as a guest blogger or a regular contributor. Consider Realtor, newspaper, and new home sites such as Atlanta Real Estate Forum, Luxury Real Estate Forum, Green Built Blog, and New Homes Section.

Custom Builders Atlanta, an affiliate of Custom Builders USA, blogs regularly on http://www.Atlanta-RealEstateForum.com. The company has gotten leads from the site and even ideas for creating a new business as a result of a connection it made through the blog.

Atlanta-based home builder Brock Built blogged on http://www.GreenBuiltBlog.com to promote an eco-friendly home the company was auctioning for charity. A producer for the local Radio Disney station read about the home on the blog and arranged to air a feature story about the home.

Form Follows Function

Blog designs vary, as the examples in this book illustrate. Free templates have basic designs, but you can create and customize more elaborate blogs. Before choosing your design, consider how it will function in the future.

In addition to current posts and an archive of previous posts, the blog should include the following:

- "About" and "contact" pages, for example
  http://www.atlantarealestateforum.com/about/
  http://www.atlantarealestateforum.com/contact/
- A disclaimer page, for example
  http://www.highlandhomes.org/news/
  disclaimer-highland-homes/

You also may want to include banner advertisements, featured news, or both. Some themes, such as those on http://www.chicagolandrealestateforum.com and http://www.luxuryrealestateforum.com, include a section for featured news or featured articles. This content appears at the top of the page, right under the masthead. Featured news does not change as frequently as the regular blog posts on these sites.

If you are considering including banner advertisements on your site, you will need to know how many unique visitors your site gets in a day, a month, and a year, and how many impressions an ad will get. The amount you can charge for ads typically depends on how much traffic your site receives. You can charge a flat rate per month or a cost per click. You also need to determine where to place ads. They can be banner ads above the *masthead* or they can be placed lower on the right or left side of the page. A builder might accept advertising for a building product or a restaurant near one of its popular communities. An HBA can accept ads from builders too. Springfield HBA (http://www.springfieldhba.com) has a number of advertisers featured on its blog/website including builders, inspection companies, design centers, and appliance resources.

Widgets, Plug-ins, and Other Gadgets

Often the words *widget* and plug-in are used almost interchangeably. They both refer to small applications of code you can install in a blog or a website after it is built. They are like car accessories. Typically these bits of codes can't function on their own but they can enhance a larger software application like the one your blog uses. Some of these widgets, plug-ins, and other gadgets add functionality and interactivity to help users engage with your site; others are management tools for you. Some of the most popular ones used with WordPress are completely invisible to users. Following are some mRELEVANCE uses:

- **All in One SEO Pack.** This is probably my all-time favorite as it allows search engine optimization to be performed on each individual blog post.

- **Akismet.** This is the ultimate spam catcher. This plug-in will check comments on your blog and sort them into a spam folder for you to review. It helps you moderate your blog in less time.
- **NextGEN Gallery.** This is an image gallery plug-in with an optional slideshow. Your visitors can view your plans, finished homes, and communities.
- **BuddyPress.** This plug-in allows you to operate your blog as a social networking site. Users can create profiles, post messages, make connections and interact between groups. RealtyJoin uses it.
- **WP-Polls.** With WP-Polls you can easily incorporate a poll into a post or a page on your blog.
- **Facebook Like.** This plug-in makes it easy for your readers to Like your content and share it with their friends.
- **Facebook Like Box Widget.** This plug-in adds an entire Facebook Like box to your blog so readers can Like your Facebook page.
- **Sociable.** This plug-in allows your readers to share the posts they like with their friends. When you configure it, you can choose from among hundreds of sites where users can share your content, including Twitter, Facebook, Digg, Delicious, Sphinn, Mixx, Posterous and many more. You can also allow readers to e-mail your posts or print PDFs of it.

You can also use plug-ins to add a calendar, your Twitter feed, a countdown timer for a big event, and many more features. You install and activate plug-ins from the WordPress dashboard. Visit WordPress (http://www.wordpress.org/extend/plugins/) to browse thousands of plug-ins. If you have ever thought, "I wish my blog could . ." it probably can. Don't get carried away with the bling, though; installing too many gadgets will distract users and make your blog slow to load and respond. You should load and activate basic plug-ins to control spam comments, generate site maps, and enhance SEO. Focus on your blog's mission and functionality.

The Magic of Keywords

Before you write your first blog post, schedule a meeting with the consultant(s) or in-house staff member(s) responsible for your website's SEO. As a group, review your website's analytics, noting the keywords the site already attracts. What are the obvious missing keywords? As you plan your keyword strategy for your blog, identify the words and phrases that your main site is not successfully attracting and ensure that your blog includes them. Blogs successfully attract long-tail keywords—typically product-specific phrases of three to five words. For instance, rather than searching for the word "car," a buyer might search for "1960 restored red Mercedes Benz."

Including the right keywords has become even more important with the release of Google Caffeine[22] and Google Instant. Released in June 2010, Google Caffeine provides 50% fresher results than previous Google indexes because it refreshes search results continuously. New optimized blog posts will appear in search results more quickly than they would have previously.

In addition to including long-tail keyword phrases in your blogs, also hone in on short keywords to bring up your company in the search results as the words are typed. Google's "Instant" feature is a search enhancement that provides results as a user is typing. For example, if a user is searching for Atlanta Real Estate, by the time they have typed "atl," Google is already offering results.

Blog Content Ideas

Stumped about what to write? Here are 10 ideas for blog posts.

1. Discuss the latest ideas for kitchen organization and demonstrate these features in a companion video.
2. Introduce your new community with a post on the top 5 reasons home buyers want to live there, including its location, amenities, quality, and value.
3. Explain your 10-point quality inspection program and videotape a mock walk-through with your construction superintendent.

4. Educate your buyers on available loan products.

5. Show and tell about available options for carpet, cabinetry, tile, and lighting, using photos or video.

6. Invite readers to an upcoming Home Show or Parade of Homes you participate in. Discuss your homes and communities and link to the show or Parade's main website with information on all the homes.

7. Videotape a testimonial from a happy homeowner. This could be a remodeling customer talking about their new kitchen (with before and after images), a new custom homeowner, or the happy family who lives in one of your planned communities. Include a photo or video testimonial to make it more real.

8. Discuss the energy-saving features that you incorporate into your homes. Explain the details about what makes new homes more energy efficient than resale homes.

9. Introduce your new colors, styles, and features for spring, summer, fall or the New Year. This works for suppliers introducing new product, builders with new plans, and designers featuring the latest trends.

10. Showcase your charity work, whether it is donating countertops to a community group home or providing a crew to finish a HomeAid house. Tell your readers how they can participate.

What Readers Want

A good blog post is written both for the consumer and for the search engines. It contains unique content, visuals (photos and video), audio, keywords, anchor text, and links. Blog posts don't have to be long; they can be 250–350 words. Video posts include a video embedded from a site such as Vimeo or YouTube and a brief written description of the video. Often these are only 150 words. Make posts conversational and interesting. Ask readers questions to start conversations. Write about topics that ignite your passions.

The most effective posts will provide the information most buyers are seeking, so describe your community's location, homes, and amenities. Readers also may want to know how to obtain financing or receive tax and energy credits.

Top 3 lists, Top 5 lists, and bulleted information attract attention. It is always a good idea to break up large blocks of text into steps or other lists using bullets in a blog post. This makes it easier for readers to absorb the information and understand what action to take. Don't forget to include a call to action in each post. For example, place a question at the end to encourage further interaction. Following are four examples of effective blog posts. Although each builder took a different approach, all four are equally engaging because they captivated readers and got them to act. Let's dig a bit further into what makes each of these a good post.

S&A Homes: Easy E-Incentive

S&A homes announced an e-incentive[23] for Realtors on its blog (fig. 3.4). The post encouraged Realtors to Like the new S&A Homes Facebook page. Each new real estate agent who liked the page and wrote a comment about working with S&A Homes received a $10 Sheetz gift card for gas. The post included three simple steps for agents to complete to get the gas card. Providing an incentive to a target audience to encourage readers to do something is also a great way to build a following among the groups you want to follow you, like Realtors.

Gerstad Builders: Educating Buyers

In addition to posting on its own news blog, McHenry County home builder Gerstad Builders frequently contributes content to http://www.ChicagolandReal EstateForum.com (fig. 3.5). The posts educate potential home buyers and drive traffic to the builder's website. For example, Gerstad contributed "4 Tips to Improve Your Credit Score."[24] The post listed the tips, quoted industry expert, Ilyce Glink, and linked to her blog at Think Glink for additional information. Using expert

Figure 3.4 **S&A Homes e-centive**

S&A Homes incentivized Realtors to Like its Facebook page.

Source: Reprinted with permission from S&A Homes, State College, Pa.

Figure 3.5 Chicagoland Real Estate Forum blog post

Gerstad Builders blogs to educate home buyers and help make the buying process easier.

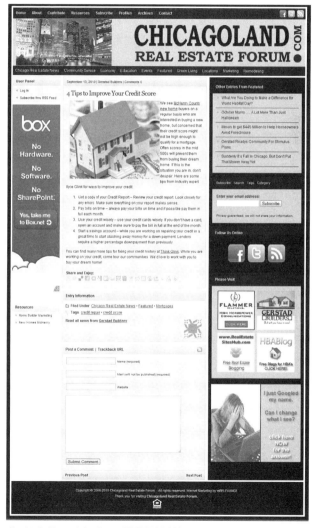

sources adds credibility to your blog posts, so interview and quote experts, and link to their sites. They may link to your post, tweet about it, or post it on Facebook.

Boone Homes: What's Not to Like?

You can use a literary device, such as irony, to engage readers on your blog and educate them about your USP. Chris Parks with Boone Homes demonstrates this with a tongue-in-cheek post titled, "The 6 ½ Best Reasons Not to Build a Boone Home."[25] For every reason he gives not to buy a Boone Home, he adds a positive counterpoint telling readers why buying one is a good idea (fig. 3.6).

Experiment to find a writing style you are comfortable with. Use titles to spark readers' curiosity.

Airing the Dirty Laundry

To elicit interaction, ask readers a question at the end of a post, or highlight an unusual or often-overlooked home feature. In the post, "Laundry—the Easy Way,"[26] Laura Spencer of Boone Homes writes about laundry room organization. Laura engages blog readers by discussing her personal experience with getting a 12-year-old to put her laundry where it belongs. Then she shows how having an organized laundry room, like those Boone Homes builds, makes laundry an easier task (fig. 3.7).

Figure 3.6 Boone Homes blog post example 1

Capture blog readers' attention with interesting headlines.

Source: Reprinted with permission from Boone Homes, Richmond, Va.

Figure 3.7 Boone Homes blog post example 2

Give readers something to relate to in your blog posts. Boone Homes does just that by talking about laundry and teenagers.

Source: Reprinted with permission from Boone Homes, Richmond, Va.

Multiple readers responded to the post thanking Laura for writing it and commenting on how small their own laundry rooms are. Do you sense there are move-up buyers here?

Use personal experiences readers can relate to and they will read your blog and, possibly, buy a home from you.

Use your blog to establish your expertise, whether it's green building, homes for first-time buyers, remodeling for aging in place, energy efficiency, interior design, mortgages, credit repair, or landscaping. Choose topics you enjoy talking about and your enthusiasm will show.

Still have writer's block? Read the paper; read other local blogs; follow top real estate agents on Trulia, ActiveRain, or Realtor.com for inspiration.

Remember what you learned in elementary school: don't plagiarize. You may reference an article with proper credit to the original source and link to it, but don't cut and paste text or images onto your site without written permission from the original author and/or the publisher.

Use your editorial calendar. Plan your posts at least a month before they are scheduled to run.

Blogging with Impact

After you write your first blog post, edit it (or better yet, ask another person to do so), and tweak it for the search engines. Make sure it includes the keywords the search engines should associate with the post. For example, if your blog post is about best plants for winter gardening, your keyword phrases might include "winter gardening," "planting during winter," or "flowers that grow in winter." Include two or three relevant keywords or keyword phrases in each blog post, but don't randomly add keywords just to try to boost your search results; your blog needs to be readable. *Stuffing* keywords into a post is content spamming: it will annoy your readers and may actually harm your search engine results.

Next, add links from your post to other sites. Links give readers the opportunity to discover additional information. For example, when a post references a company or organization, hyperlink its name to its website. Also consider incorporating your company's keywords as anchor text. For example, if you referenced Orange County townhomes in a post, you would link the words "Orange County townhomes" to the community page on your website that discusses the townhomes. Each blog post should have one to three links to other sites. At least one of these should go to a page on your main website, but rather than always linking to your home page, regularly link to other pages within the site. Consider linking to previous posts to your blog as well. If your post references a topic or event discussed in a previous post, link to that post.

Keep It Fresh

More than 95% of blogs are abandoned.[27] Launching a blog is a major commitment. You must be dedicated and willing to post consistently. There is nothing worse than stale content. When a site visitor clicks on an events page only to find last year's events, they are frustrated and your brand is tarnished. You don't want to eat stale cereal, and neither do your readers. Determine how often you can post; create an editorial calendar, and stick to it.

If the main goal of your blog is SMO, plan to post two times per week. By varying the day and time of each post you will keep the search engines coming back to your site more often in search of fresh content. This is generally a good dose of content for readers, too—just enough to keep them coming back, but not enough to overwhelm them.

Managing a Blog

One individual should manage the blog, although various authors can write or contribute other content to it. The blog manager could be an employee or whoever handles your marketing or PR. The blog manager will

- oversee the blog schedule;
- review the editorial content;
- ensure that writers post content regularly; and
- moderate the blog.

The moderator will ensure posts contain keywords, anchor text, and links; monitor and respond to comments; and forward comments that require a response to the appropriate individual.

Because they offer a variety of perspectives and voices, some of the most interesting blogs have multiple authors. However, readers expect transparency, so tell them who is blogging on your corporate site. Consider having the president, marketing director, real estate agents, and others contribute. Create an individual profile for each blogger so a writer can build his or her own personal brand and voice. Invite guest bloggers to post on your site.

Time

Budget 20 hours a month for eight posts. Each blog post will probably take at least an hour to write, depending on how much research the topic requires and whether you will have to search for a visual. Plan another 30 minutes for your blog manager to moderate each post.

Follow Copyright Law

Just because content is posted online does not mean that you can copy and paste it to your own blog. Like other published works, online content is covered by copyright law. Cutting and pasting stories from your daily newspaper, business journal, favorite social media, real estate blog, or any other website violates the law. You can reference, quote from, or paraphrase material that you see or read online by following "fair use" guidelines that go hand in hand with copyright law. However, be cautious in doing so, especially when you are using the material for commercial purposes. Acknowledging the source of the copyrighted material does not substitute for obtaining permission and no specific number of words, lines, or notes may legally be taken without permission.[28] To protect yourself, get written permission if you want to republish material. For more information on fair use, visit the U.S. Copyright Office online at http://www.copyright.gov.

In addition, be aware that search engines like Google try to index pages of distinct information, and they will index the first or the most relevant post when there is identical content. So, even if you get permission to use information from another site, it is not a good SEO strategy. In fact, a search engine may remove from its index a site with redundant material.[29] It will no longer appear in search results.

Photos

Copyrights apply to photos and illustrations as well as written work. Penalties can be as high as $20,000 per image, not to mention court costs. If you want to use others' content, first verify that it is available for you to use under the *Creative Commons license*. This copyright license permits distribution of others' content within specific guidelines.

If you find valuable content that you want to reference, mention it (rather than copying and pasting it) and be sure to credit the original source, which may be different from the website where you found the material. You can discuss why you like the content, paraphrasing one or two main points, and its relevance for potential home buyers. Then write your own conclusion, in your own words, to your post.

Promoting Your Blog

If you build it, they will come—but only in the movies. So avoid living in a field of dreams and, instead, tirelessly promote your blog. Invite readers to sign up for your e-mail or RSS feed or read your blog through their preferred feed. This is like subscribing to a newspaper or newsletter, but readers get to choose how their content is delivered.

Netweave all of your Internet marketing. This means including a link to your blog on your website, in your e-mail signature, on your banner ads, in your e-mail marketing, on your social networking sites, and anywhere else you can find a place to include a link or an icon.

Format your blog to tweet your latest post and use Networked Blogs (*see* Resources) to connect your blog to your Facebook fan page.

Commenting on other people's related blogs is a great way to attract visitors to your blog. For example, if you are a green builder, comment on various green blogs. Just ensure your comments are relevant, and not spam.

Finally, register your blog with blog directories Technorati and Blog Catalog.

S&A homes (http://www.SAHomesBlog.com) does an excellent job of netweaving. Its blog's home page prominently displays links to the company's social media sites and to a form users can complete to subscribe to the blog. The blog features a video from the builder's YouTube channel on its the home page (fig. 3.8). Sociable icons placed at the bottom of each blog post encourage readers to share their favorite content.

Tracking Users

To gauge whether your blog is meeting expectations for unique visitors, how much time they spend on the site, and the number of pages they visit, you need tracking software. Most blogging platforms offer at least a rudimentary tool for this. For a self-hosted WordPress blog, use Google Analytics to track performance.

Figure 3.8 S&A Homes blog

S&A Homes prominently features video on the home page of its blog.

Source: Reprinted with permission from S&A Homes, State College, Pa.

Review tracking data monthly, noting month-over-month and year-over-year trends. Besides being able to measure your blog's success, you will be able to see cyclical patterns in online real estate traffic. Note the following data:

- **Number of unique visitors to your blog.** What is the proportion of returning visitors to new visitors?
- **Average time each visitor spends on your site.** If your blog is a strong *referral site* to your main website, this number may be low (from a half-second to a minute or so).
- **Number of pages (posts) that each visitor goes to.** If the page count is low, consider that some visitors may be leaving the blog to visit your company's website.
- **Referring sites.** These are the sites your blog visitors are coming from. Facebook, Twitter, and other websites where you have promoted your blog should be sending you visitors.
- **Keyword searches.** You can count the number of times keywords in your blog actually were typed into search engines and which keywords in your posts were most popular.
- **Most popular content.** You can gauge readers' interests by the pages they land on, where they spend most of their time, and the pages from which they exit your blog.

- **Visitors.** Use the map overlay feature to display the geographic region your traffic is coming from. For example, http://www.AtlantaRealEstateForum.com had traffic from all 50 states in a 30-day period.

Your main website's analytics also reveal how well your blog performs. An effective blog will emerge as a top referral source to the company's main website and will send quality referral traffic to the website. If your blog is separate from your website, here's what you want to look for:

- **Increased traffic.** Typically, companies will get a 20% boost in traffic or more after launching a blog and optimizing their websites, but some mRelevance clients have seen growth of 200%–600%.
- **Increase in referring sites.** Because of syndication and cross-promotion of your web presence, your blog should be among the top 5 referral sources to your main website.
- **Keywords.** The list of keywords will expand if you are blogging with keywords as anchor text.

If your blog and website are built on the same platform you will need to gauge the ROI a bit differently. At a minimum, note keywords, time on site, and referring sites. Each of these metrics should show year-over-year increases.

You should gain at least three other measurable ROIs from your online efforts:

1. **SERP.** When you Google your name or other keyword phrases, you should start to see more of your results on page one.
2. **Enhanced brand.** Your company will be recognized as readily online as in print.
3. **Increased efficiency.** Your blog will reduce the amount of time you spend feeding your social media program by integrating your blog with your website and social media activities. Instead of posting the same material three or four times on different sites, you can write one blog post, check off the other sites where you want the material to appear, and post brief comments on social media sites between your blog posts.

Troubleshooting

If your blog isn't a top referral source for your main website within 30–60 days of launch, one of four problems may be to blame:

1. **Infrequent posting.** When was the last time you posted? If it was 90 days ago or even 3 weeks ago, you aren't giving your readers or the search engines a reason to come back.

2. **Dull content.** Make sure your content is compelling to your readers. Is it fun and informative? If it isn't, then spice it up!

3. **Lack of promotion.** Does your blog have an RSS feed? Did you connect it to Facebook and Twitter? Have you let your customers know where to find it? Did you register it on blog directories?

4. **Poor construction.** Does the blog contain hard code that breaks the theme? WordPress themes are a combination of files that work together to create a blog's design and functionality. Themes can be configured many ways to allow for unique design. However, if a web developer or someone else adds HTML code in the wrong place, your theme will not work as intended.

5. **Wrong or no SEO tools.** Make sure you have installed an SEO plug-in, like the All in One SEO plug-in. Check to see if you are using an XML sitemap plug-in as well.

The blog is the one tool in your social media toolbox that you own. Social networks will come and go. The content you post on them isn't cataloged or sortable, and, in most cases, isn't indexed by Google. Most importantly, the content you post on social networks really isn't yours. The social media sites can (and will) change their policies and take profiles and accounts down at any time and for any reason. Even free online blog accounts are vulnerable to disappearing. Ensuring your company has a reasonable amount of control over its image and reputation becomes more and more challenging as online social media channels expand their reach.

Online Public Relations

An online public relations strategy augments your traditional PR program. Instead of interacting with the public through traditional media and events, online PR provides an avenue not only for SEO, but also to reach multiple target audiences directly, including members of the media. A study by Brunswick Research[30] found that more than two-thirds of journalists have written a story about something they found through social media. The study focused on the trends in the use of social media by global business journalists. Key findings include:

- Social media is increasing as an influential source of information used by journalists.
- Social media has a positive effect on the quality of journalism, including the angle and content of stories.
- Nine out of 10 journalists have used social media to investigate an issue.

- Twitter provides the most valuable information sources but blogs often provide a foundation for a story.
- North American journalists use and believe in social media more than journalists in other locations do.
- 72% of journalists said social media will play an increasing role in their profession.
- 25% get information from online public relations distribution services, other online subscriptions, and Google Alerts.

A Middleberg/Ross study[31] found that 98% of journalists go online daily searching for news:

- 92% research articles on the web
- 76% look for new expert sources on the web.
- 73% use the Internet to find press releases.

Online PR allows you to control your messages. By incorporating keywords, anchor text, and links in your online news releases, you transform them into a powerful SMO tool. Google "Gerstad Builders" to see how one builder has filled its search results with a combination of blogs, online PR, and its own website.

Another recent poll[32] found that 89% of journalists depend on social media for story research:

- 89% use blogs for story research;
- 65% use social networking sites;

- 52% use microblogging sites like Twitter; and
- 61% use information from Wikipedia.

One major concern that journalists expressed is the information on these sites is often unreliable. Because online media greatly influence traditional media, businesses can extend their reach by using online channels. By posting stories online, you can become the expert source journalists discover in their Internet searches. Press releases will contribute positively to your SEO because you can place links to your website in them. Many sites designed to distribute online press releases also allow keyword anchor text. Both paid and free websites allow businesses to post online press releases (*see* Resources). Shop these companies to determine which will suit your needs. Some will display releases online and e-mail them to reporters. PRWeb.com (fig. 4.1) and pitchengine.com are great options for the budget-conscious. Choose services that allow you to incorporate links and anchor text in your press releases.

Top Three Ways to Distribute Content

You have timely, newsworthy information about your newest community, product, sales successes, or new plans. How do you distribute it? You can use two traditional

Figure 4.1 PRWeb.com

PRWeb is one of many online press release distribution services.

methods of verbally pitching your story to the media or e-mailing a press release. You can also use a third option–social media–to get the word out.

1. **Pitching.** Pitching is still a very effective way to get a major media outlet to cover your story. Often newspapers and other media don't want to compete with each other for stories. By pitching the story as an exclusive to just one reporter you have the opportunity for more in-depth coverage of your story. Once the story runs, you can release it to other publications and post it online. The key to pitching and scoring is to understand the reporter you are pitching to. Avoid calling them when you know they are on deadline and understand their publication and the types of stories they will cover. Don't throw them a curve ball with an unrelated pitch. Pitches are best reserved for major news. Your new community with 50 deposits for homes that are not yet built is worth pitching.

2. **Press Releases.** A PR staple, the press release is still a crucial part of telling your story to the media. Press releases are an excellent way to reach many news outlets simultaneously. We usually use press releases for features, rather than news stories. The grand opening of your new community, a new product, or a new floorplan are suitable for a press release.

3. **Social Media.** This is the newest venue for distributing content. It's fast, you can reach millions of people with a single mouse click, and it places your company news in the venue that most people are using. From online press releases to blogging, social media provides an instant platform for your information. Plus, you can incorporate SEO to launch your content to the top of the news agenda and burst through the noise.

How to Write a Press Release

Contact information (name, telephone number, e-mail address) appears at the top of the page. The headline comes next. It clearly states what the release is about and is usually centered in bold type. Include the location of the news in a *dateline* preceding the text of the news release. The first paragraph should catch the reader's attention and answer: who, what, where, when, why, and how. It should contain a news peg, telling the readers why they should care about the topic right now.

The second and third paragraphs should provide more details and at least one quote from a person relevant to the news story. When you quote this *source,* use their full name with a complete identification, which includes their title or position and company. Quotes allow you to add a positive endorsement to a press release. For example, if your model home just won an award, you may refer to the award and use phrases such as "award-winning community" in your press release and then describe the classic architecture or modern décor. However, if you want to insert opinion into the release, such as a statement that the home is "beautiful" or "outstanding" or "the best value," you'll need to put it in a quote.

Boilerplate text that describes your company, similar to an *elevator speech,* should follow the news story. Include your website's and social media site's URLs. This text should be part of your press release template because you will only update it as needed, rather than creating a new "speech" for every release.

Figure 4.2 shows a press release in the proper format.

After your press release is written, revisit your list of keywords and incorporate a few of them into the release. Use them on sites that allow anchor text to link to your website or your blog. Most marketers who are not versed in it overlook this method of SEO.

When you are submitting press releases directly to media outlets, you should only distribute information that is truly newsworthy. If you constantly send press releases to the media that they do not deem newsworthy, reporters and editors will ignore your e-mail messages. On the other hand, although reporters may not find your latest sales incentive newsworthy (considering it advertising, rather than news), online consumers probably will. Go ahead and write it up for online distribution. In addition, don't think

Figure 4.2 Press release

A press release includes contact information, a bold headline, a dateline, keywords, and your elevator speech.

RealtyJoin®

RELEASE DATE:
March 8, 2011

CONTACT:
mRELEVANCE
Carol Flammer: 770-383-3360 x20
Carol@mRELEVANCE.com

RealtyJoin Launches Version 2.0 - An Enhanced Social Marketplace

ATLANTA – RealtyJoin, a free interactive social and business networking site for the real estate industry in the United States and Canada, announces the launch of version 2.0. This totally redesigned real estate social networking site does everything that the original version of RealtyJoin did, only better. The new, enhanced RealtyJoin website is a social marketplace for the entire real estate industry where individuals can connect, network and advertise potential opportunities.

RealtyJoin 2.0 offers a more user-friendly integrated website that includes WordPress blogs for all users, upgraded navigation, enhanced profiles, video options, upcoming events, the ability to post status updates, photos and video.

"We decided to start RealtyJoin because we saw that real estate investors, REALTORS®, tradespeople, home builders and designers were looking for good, Internet-based tools to help them network, find and advertise opportunities," said Andy Heller, a veteran real estate investor and public speaker, as well as RealtyJoin co-founder. "Our site is a community for real estate agents, investors, plumbers and electricians, stagers, home builders and anyone who believes that the free exchange of information will increase sales."

Ilyce Glink, an award-winning, nationally syndicated columnist, blogger, bestselling author and radio talk show host recently joined the RealtyJoin team to oversee content strategy. Glink says she has been impressed with RealtyJoin's ability to connect individuals and offer them the ability to share pertinent industry related content.

"In just a few short months, RealtyJoin proved there is a real need for a place where real estate investors and the companies they work with can connect and share information," she said. A number of high profile real estate groups and associations are participating in RealtyJoin, including the Atlanta Board of Realtors®, Foreclosure.com, Southeast Valley Regional Association of Realtors®, and RIS Media.

RealtyJoin offers the real estate industry an opportunity to gain business traction by starting online conversations and relationship with buyers, sellers, architects, contractors, brokers, suppliers and other professionals.

The introductory level of RealtyJoin remains free. Premium and executive memberships will be available over the next several months for those seeking further upgrades and enhancements.

For more information on RealtyJoin 2.0 and to join the premiere social marketplace of the real estate industry, visit www.RealtyJoin.com. "Like" RealtyJoin on Facebook at www.facebook.com/ RealtyJoin and follow RealtyJoin on Twitter at http://twitter.com/RealtyJoin.

# # #

that all stories must be time sensitive. Many builders have lifestyle or feature stories without an immediate expiration date that are perfect for online distribution. Although your news peg in evergreen stories may not tell the reader why the story is timely, it should still capture their attention and motivate them to keep reading by showing how the story is important or useful.

Post press releases to your website's press room as they are released. Your online newsroom should be easily accessible from your home page. Consider adding it into the main navigation as a "News" tab or as part of the drop-down menu under "About." Your online newsroom should contain a corporate backgrounder and/or corporate fact sheet, recent press releases, and your corporate logo (see http://www.wilsonparkerhomes.com/atlanta-new-homes/press-room.php.).

Press releases should display in reverse chronological order so that reporters and consumers can easily find the most recent news. If you have videos you want to make available to reporters, add those to your newsroom as well.

If uploading releases to your main website is cumbersome, consider adding a press section to your blog and uploading them there instead.

As company press releases accumulate online, Google your name. You will probably like what you see!

PRnewswire.com and BusinessWire.com are the oldest and most established sites in online public relations. They had established relationships with media outlets long before social media was invented. Both do an excellent job of targeting reporters and populating the Internet with a number of stories within an hour or so of release. Their per-release fees vary depending on the number of words, media lists targeted, and whether a photo is included and/or archived. The Daybook service, available in Atlanta, Dallas, and Nashville, also has delivered consistently positive results. NHDbuzz. com (fig. 4.3), a subsidiary of New Homes Directory, places press releases at no cost as a service to the new home industry. The site also features a Q&A section, "Ask Carol," where you can get answers to public relations and social media questions (fig. 4.4).

Online PR: An Extension of Traditional PR

Soleil Laurel Canyon, a resort-inspired active adult community in Canton, Georgia, developed by Active Lifestyle Communities, uses online public relations to expand its traditional public relations strategy. A number of online press release sites provide consistent referral traffic to the community's website, http://www.SoleilLaurel Canyon.com. Sites such as Atlanta Daybook, PRLog, and dBusiness News consistently help consumers find more information on this community and click through to

Figure 4.3 NHD Buzz

You can post online news stories for free at NHD Buzz.

Ashton Woods Homes Sees Sales Success at Madison Park

Monday, April 04, 2011 / Ashton Woods Homes

Ashton Woods Homes is pleased to announce it sales success at Madison Park, a community of single family homes in Johns Creek. Since 2010, 47 homes were sold making this the fastest-selling community in the area.

Only three homes remain at Madison Park, including the model home. The model includes luxury upgrades and is priced at $474,900. All homes at Madison Park offer impressive architecture, with four-sides-brick exteriors on the main level, carriage style garage doors and uniquely designed interiors with more than 3,200 square feet. Homes also include energy performance features that can save up to 40 percent on homeowners' utility expenses.

Madison Park is walking distance to parks, restaurants, shops cafes and grocery stores. It is also only a live to ten minute drive to North Point Mall. Madison Park is convenient to Georgia 400 as well as numerous country clubs and Lake Lanier.

Children residing in Madison Park attend Barnwell Elementary, Autry Mill Middle and Johns Creek High schools.

The model home is open daily: Sunday and Monday from noon to 6 p.m. and Tuesday through Saturday from 10 a.m. to 6 p.m.

To visit Madison Park, travel Georgia 400 North to Exit 9, Haynes Bridge Road. Go right off the exit. Drive 2.7 miles and turn left on Old Alabama Road. Madison Park will be .8 of a mile on the left.

For more information on the community, visit www.ashtonwoods.com/atlanta or call 678-366-0431.

About Ashton Woods Homes:

Ashton Woods Homes is one of the nation's largest private homebuilding companies with operations in Orlando, Tampa, Atlanta, Raleigh, Dallas, Houston, Austin and Phoenix. Homes built by Ashton Woods are designed to complement a diverse range of lifestyles and offer the energy-efficiency, luxury, quality and value you'd expect from one of the nations premier new home builders. For more information, visit www.ashtonwoodshomes.com.

Other Information:
For more Atlanta real estate news, visit Atlanta Real Estate Forum.

Published by: Carol Flammer
mRELEVANCE, LLC is a public relations, Internet marketing and social media firm designed to meet client needs in a changing marketplace by building online and offline relationships that are relevant to client success. Combining the talents and resources of public relations and social media firm Flammer Relations with the power of Internet marketing services at MLC New Home Marketing, mRELEVANCE implements a combination of traditional PR services and up-to-date Web 2.0 tools (e-mail marketing, search engine optimization, social media and others) to create relevant results for clients.
770-383-3360 http://www.mRELEVANCE.com This article has been viewed 21 time(s).

Related Articles :
No Related Content Found

🖨 PRINT   ✉ EMAIL

Share this article on LinkedIn

Report this article as abuse

Reviews : 0   User Rating :

Submit your Review

Source: Reprinted with permission from NHD Buzz, Murrieta, California

Figure 4.4 "Ask Carol" Q&A

Ask Carol answers questions about PR and Social Media.

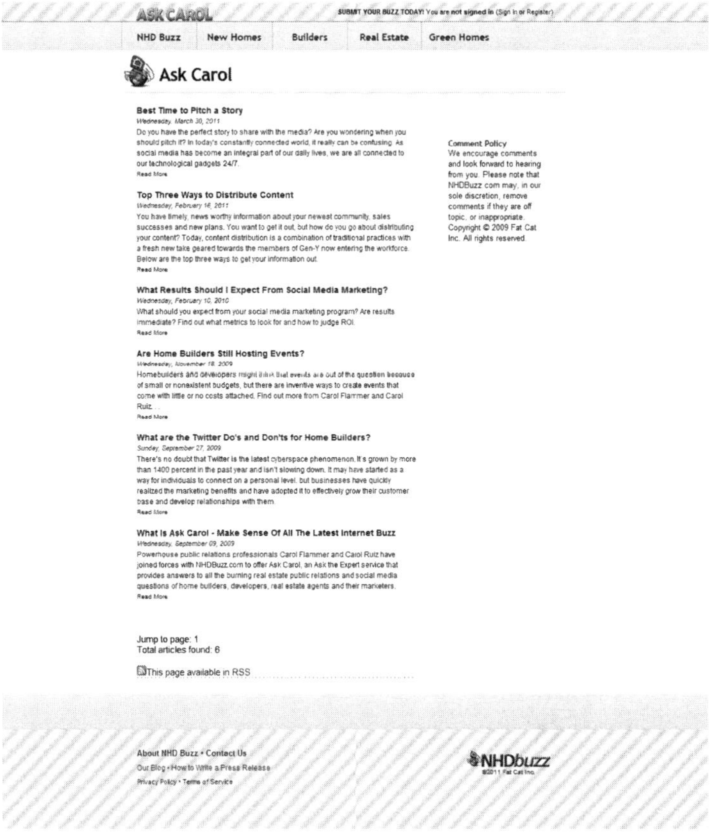

ASK CAROL

SUBMIT YOUR BUZZ TODAY! You are not signed in (Sign In or Register)

NHD Buzz | New Homes | Builders | Real Estate | Green Homes

Ask Carol

Best Time to Pitch a Story
Wednesday, March 30, 2011
Do you have the perfect story to share with the media? Are you wondering when you should pitch it? In today's constantly connected world, it really can be confusing. As social media has become an integral part of our daily lives, we are all connected to our technological gadgets 24/7.
Read More

Top Three Ways to Distribute Content
Wednesday, February 16, 2011
You have timely, news worthy information about your newest community, sales successes and new plans. You want to get it out, but how do you go about distributing your content? Today, content distribution is a combination of traditional practices with a fresh new take geared towards the members of Gen-Y now entering the workforce. Below are the top three ways to get your information out.
Read More

What Results Should I Expect From Social Media Marketing?
Wednesday, February 10, 2010
What should you expect from your social media marketing program? Are results immediate? Find out what metrics to look for and how to judge ROI.
Read More

Are Home Builders Still Hosting Events?
Wednesday, November 18, 2009
Homebuilders and developers might think that events are out of the question because of small or nonexistent budgets, but there are inventive ways to create events that come with little or no costs attached. Find out more from Carol Flammer and Carol Ruiz. . .
Read More

What are the Twitter Do's and Don'ts for Home Builders?
Sunday, September 27, 2009
There's no doubt that Twitter is the latest cyberspace phenomenon. It's grown by more than 1400 percent in the past year and isn't slowing down. It may have started as a way for individuals to connect on a personal level, but businesses have quickly realized the marketing benefits and have adopted it to effectively grow their customer base and develop relationships with them.
Read More

What Is Ask Carol - Make Sense Of All The Latest Internet Buzz
Wednesday, September 09, 2009
Powerhouse public relations professionals Carol Flammer and Carol Ruiz have joined forces with NHDBuzz.com to offer Ask Carol, an Ask the Expert service that provides answers to all the burning real estate public relations and social media questions of home builders, developers, real estate agents and their marketers.
Read More

Jump to page: 1
Total articles found: 6

This page available in RSS

Comment Policy
We encourage comments and look forward to hearing from you. Please note that NHDBuzz.com may, in our sole discretion, remove comments if they are off topic, or inappropriate. Copyright © 2009 Fat Cat Inc. All rights reserved.

About NHD Buzz • Contact Us
Our Blog • How to Write a Press Release
Privacy Policy • Terms of Service

NHDbuzz
©2011 Fat Cat Inc.

Source: Reprinted with permission from NHD Buzz, Murrieta, California

the website. One of the community's top referral sources is LiveSouth. Its website traffic spikes after e-blasts that promote the Soleil news on LiveSouth.

Becoming an Expert Source

In addition to populating keyword search results with press releases demonstrating your company's expertise, you can also take advantage of a free online service to review and respond to reporter queries. Help A Reporter Out (HARO) was started in 2008 by serial entrepreneur and social media guru Peter Shankman. Almost 30,000 reporters from local, regional, national and international media outlets (*Huffington Post, USA Today, New York Times*, television news shows, Internet outlets and more) post queries related to stories they are researching, and subscribing sources respond when they can help. Each weekday, subscribers receive several e-mails throughout the day with queries organized by general topic areas, including real estate. Many subscribing sources also follow HARO on Twitter and Facebook to receive up-to-the-minute queries.

To become a subscribing source, visit http://helpare porter.com. When you sign up, you will agree to respond to queries only when you have relevant information, and you will agree not to contact any reporter you find on

HARO with unrelated news. That means you may not add the reporter to any e-mail list without permission (the list's strict adherence to privacy policies is one thing that attracts reporters and keeps them coming back).

When you find a query you can answer, simply follow the instructions to respond. You will have the most success when you offer succinct information. The reporter will follow up with questions if needed (don't be surprised if you don't get a response).

HARO queries often include deadlines, and it's vital that you meet these. If the query generates too many responses for the reporter to handle, responses will be capped, so it's best to respond early. If the reporter follows up with you, respond quickly. Reporters are more likely to build long-term relationships with sources they can count on to be timely and accurate.

If you would like to proactively position your company's leaders as experts in their fields, well-placed links on Twitter, Facebook, and Linkedin can help build respect and trust. However, if members of the media aren't among your friends, fans, or followers, you may not be reaching the right audience to garner publicity. Although social media is the newest way to connect, attracting members of the press to join the groups that receive your social media messages usually requires old-fashioned networking and relationship building.

If your company leaders can speak knowledgeably about a local current event, call a reporter; but first organize and rehearse some talking points so they can speak logically and concisely about the issue. Writing a letter to the editor or a guest editorial in the local newspaper or securing speaking engagements at local community groups are additional traditional ways of establishing expertise.

After a media outlet features your company, don't forget to extend the impact of the publicity by posting links to the story on your blog and website pressroom.

What Qualifies as News?

Different media outlets, including online outlets, view the newsworthiness of stories differently. Sometimes your company's news will stand alone. Other times, you may be part of a bigger story, such as a "trend" story on the housing market, home design, or community revitalization. Becoming part of larger news stories is never guaranteed, but several strategies already discussed in this chapter will help reporters find you and remember you: old-fashioned networking and relationship-building, registering as a source for HARO queries, and publishing press releases with keywords. Although the first two methods require proactively reaching out to reporters (only under the right conditions on HARO), the latter one helps reporters find you if they're searching for a particular topic online. You will want to make sure you have plenty of online releases incorporating lots of relevant keywords so reporters can find you when they need you.

What kind of news should you publish? Following are typical topics home builders address in their press releases:

- Community groundbreaking or opening
- New model home
- Innovative floor plan or exterior design
- Green building or other specialized construction method
- Charitable activity
- Personnel change (new hire or promotion in key positions)
- Award (to a person or for a product)
- Achievement of professional designation

Whenever you can demonstrate innovation or show that you are setting a trend, excelling, or bringing change in the community, you have a story!

Building Relationships with Reporters

Old-fashioned face-to-face networking or getting online introductions through sites like Linkedin will help you get to know reporters. Old-fashioned customer service will keep them coming back. As with any customer relationship, you'll want to show them that you understand their needs and concerns. This means being accurate and timely, and providing the best possible product, such as written information and photos, that you can.

Once the relationship is established, they may follow your Twitter feed or fan your Facebook page. Attracting media coverage of your company requires the same tenacity as attracting home buyers does.

Social Networking

Social networking engages others in online conversation. You need the right friends, fans, and followers to network with just as you network face to face. Although social networking is fun, don't lose sight of your program's foundation—your blog—in the excitement of the social networking party.

Social Networking Sites

Facebook

Twitter

YouTube

Trulia

ActiveRain

Linkedin

Flickr

Facebook

Facebook is a 24/7 cocktail party with 130 (for the average Facebook user) of your closest friends. Half of Facebook users log on to the site daily. The average Facebook user is connected to 80 community pages, groups, and events. They are willing to Like your corporate fan page if you provide them with information that interests them.

Facebook is a tool for building a personal brand—or destroying your reputation. Using your personal profile, you can reconnect with old friends and make new ones. As your friends change their "status," you receive updates on your wall. Facebook users can add photos, video, and other content to their personal pages; choose their desired level of security; and build a network of connections. Before you can launch a business fan page or a group, you must first have a personal profile. Facebook is built on the premise that you are a person first and then as a person you can have a corporate page. Remember your corporation is not a person. Therefore, do not launch your corporate page as a person. Not only is this against Facebook policy, it also limits the applications you can use to interact with various audiences.

Creating Your Personal Profile

Complete your profile.

- Enter contact information
  - ○ Name (consider incorporating your maiden name)

○ Photo (a casual but appropriate photo is best)
○ URLs for your website, blog, Linkedin, etc.
○ Phone numbers
○ E-mail addresses
● Current and former companies
● Education

Get your Facebook URL http://www.Facebook.com/username (after you have 25 friends visit this page to secure the URL for your name). This is the equivalent of getting a vanity license plate. It allows you to easily give your Facebook address to your friends and business connections.

Customize your privacy settings. There are many levels of privacy. You can keep your profile hidden, available only to friends, or wide open to the world. Most Facebook users choose a privacy level somewhere in the middle.

Posting to Your Personal Page

After building your personal page, decide how often to post and what to post.

● Will your page be designed for friends and family?
● What content do you want to share?
● Will you post photos?

If you choose to keep your page personal, remember to share business news occasionally with your Facebook friends. You don't want to miss a great referral because one of your friends isn't thinking about what you do for a living! Whether you choose to friend personal, professional, or a combination of contacts, think carefully about what you are posting. Would you say it to your grandmother? If not, save it for a private conversation. Although you may be using Facebook's privacy settings and direct messaging vigorously, you are still on a public site. Always consider carefully what you intend to post online before you add content.

Encourage interaction among Facebook friends by tagging (or identifying) people in posts and in photos. To tag your post, type the @ symbol followed by a Facebook friend's name (without a space between them). For example, type @JohnDoe. Tagging causes your post to show up in their feed and encourages conversations and interactions. When you engage others, your information will appear more often in their feeds. If you are posting for business purposes, you want to appear in your friends' "Top News" to increase your visibility.

You can share content and spark interaction on Facebook in other ways too: add video, incorporate your blog, play a game, create an event, join causes.

Facebook Do's

- Use your real name and photo.
- Choose your profile photo wisely (keep it professional or neutral).
- Complete your biography thoughtfully. When you list your birthday, block the year for security reasons.
- Review your privacy settings.
- Join groups.
- Consider your tone.
- Interact, comment, converse.

Facebook Don'ts

- Share personal information publicly.
- Hit "reply all" in group e-mails.
- Feel like you have to friend everyone, join every group, or respond to every invitation to join a page.
- Announce where you are going—*cyberstalkers* may be watching to see when you are out of town.
- Set up your business as a person.

The Fan Page

Creating a Facebook fan page gives your company the opportunity to build a fan base of people who Like your business. Once you have fans, you'll want to communicate with them regularly and find ways to engage them in conversations. Determine your audience and what to talk about. If you are a remodeler specializing in aging in place, your page could focus on safety concerns for seniors and easy remodels that allow homeowners to enjoy their homes more as they age. A custom builder might discuss steps for choosing or designing a house plan or how to select a custom builder. All businesses should include customer testimonials.

Having the right fans is critical to success with Facebook. If everyone you are following is another builder, you are not speaking to potential home buyers. Home builders who are successful on Facebook have built relationships with co-op real estate agents or existing homeowners who are happy to cheer their favorite builder. Think about the target audience(s) with whom you can successfully interact on Facebook, seek them out, and start conversations with them.

Boone Homes, of Richmond and Roanoke, Va., (http://www.Facebook.com/boonehomesva), posts interesting news, incentive offers, upcoming events, and information about restaurants in the communities where it builds. This helps home shoppers get to know a community before they buy. Simply having a profile on Facebook and pushing your messages out isn't enough to build your brand, though. You need a team member who fully embraces the medium. He or she could be the *online sales counselor,* receptionist, marketing director, real estate agent, or a family member. As you build your Facebook presence, the leader of your effort should strive to find three to five new fans daily and interact with them. As your presence solidifies, find creative ways to engage the fans that Like you in conversation on your Facebook wall.

Creating the Fan Page

Choose your category carefully from among the many available options because you can't change it once you have created the page. Your choice may be different from others' in the same profession. Some options are

- Local: real estate
- Local: other business
- Local: home service
- Brand, product, or organization: home living

Also choose your name thoughtfully. Because the search engines index these pages you might want to incorporate keywords in the name of the fan page like this: "Sterling custom homes–Austin custom home builder."

Building Out the Fan Page

Include your logo, website URL, phone numbers, and links to other social media sites.

Add Facebook applications:

- **A blog.** Use Networked Blogs, notes, or an RSS feed.
- **Twitter.** If you are not a high-volume tweeter, consider having your Twitter account post tweets on your Facebook page. On the other hand, if you tweet frequently, using a tool such as Selective Tweets allows you to integrate your Facebook and Twitter accounts without over-whelming your fans and followers. Simply add #fb to the end of tweets that you want to appear on Facebook.
- **Video.** Add video to your site via YouTube or another video application.
- **Photos.** Add photos directly to your page or im-port them via Flickr or another application (peo-ple love viewing pictures of homes, events, and other homeowners).
- **Tabs.** Add tabs to your Facebook page to greatly expand your ability to interact with fans who Like your page. You can build tabs using *HTML, Java Script,* or *CSS.* For those with less technical know-how, Facebook has built-in applications (some free and some fee based) to help you create a tab. Facebook has changed how it will handle these pages.

Stay up to date on new requirements by reading blogs, such as http://www.Mashable.com, that follow and blog about Facebook changes.

Finding Fans

After you build your page, add content, and have posts, you must find fans. Most Facebook users will visit your page to review it for relevant content before they decide whether or not to Like it. You may want to provide an incentive for them to Like your page. From a $10 coupon to a percentage off upgrades on new homes, builders are finding fun ways to reward and encourage fans to Like them on Facebook. According to *Advertising Age,* Facebook has become the "loyalty card of the Internet."[33] Give your buyers ways to embrace you. You can promote your Facebook fan page to friends and prospective clients in four primary ways:

1. **Suggest to friends.** Click "suggest to friends" (under the profile photo at the upper left) and click your friends to select them. Once they Like your Fan page you will not be able to click them; this prevents you from asking them more than once.

2. **Post to your wall.** Click the "share" button (bottom left). Write a comment, such as "Please Like my page for great incentives." Choose who you want to share with from the drop-down list beside the

padlock (everyone, friends and networks, friends of friends, etc). Click share.

3. **Share via Facebook e-mail or other e-mail.** Click the "share" button (bottom left). Choose "send a message" to ask a friend or prospective buyer to Like your Fan page. You also can ask a friend or a list of friends to join by including a personal message. The message you send can be an e-mail or Facebook message. This method works well if you have a list of e-mail addresses for people who may or may not be active on Facebook.

4. **Use coupons and contests.** Builders have created clever campaigns to get various audiences to Like their page for a chance to download a coupon or win a gift card. This strategy, combined with e-blasts and blog promotions, can quickly build a fan base.

Another way to promote your Facebook page is to mention it on the pages of related groups or on other corporate pages. When you join a group or Like a corporate page, you can usually post to its wall. This is a great way to cross promote upcoming events, but know the group's policies before posting. Group moderators may consider your post spam and delete it, or they may report you to Facebook.

After your page has 25 fans, you can get your fan page URL. Go to http://www.Facebook.com/username

to secure a unique name. This is important for two reasons: (1) the search engines index page URLs—you want yours to appear when prospective buyers search for your name, and (2) you can add it to your printed collateral.

You also may want to explore Facebook groups. If you host many events, a group page may serve you better than a fan page. However, most home builders, remodelers, and brokers will find that a fan page offers the best options for their social media marketing goals. The two types of Facebook pages offer slightly different functionality.

Creating Events

Creating events on Facebook is not only easy, it's fun! From the Events tab on your fan page, click the "create event" button. Include important details such as contact information for visitors who have questions, whether there is a fee to participate in the event, and whether it requires an RSVP (and how to respond). You can choose to show the guest list on the event page or keep it private. You also can choose whether or not to display RSVPs.

Promoting Your Facebook Page

After you have a Facebook page, you must tell people about it! List your Facebook page on your website, blog, e-mail signature, Linkedin, and in other communications. You can use the Facebook icon or include a text link to the page. Another easy way to promote your Facebook page is to write about it on your blog or talk about it in your e-mail newsletter. Add it to your advertising as well.

Getting Fans

Homebuyers Like you on Facebook because they want something in return. You will keep them as fans if you provide them with a reason to Like you. You could announce your events and sales on Facebook first, or provide them with a coupon for the purchase of a new home. Lakeland, Florida-based Highland Homes created a Facebook coupon that encouraged visitors to Like their page (fig. 5.1). The coupon offered a discount on options from the company's Personal Selection Studio. It provided for a 20% or a 10% discount, depending on when buyers purchased their new homes. Twelve coupons were redeemed.

S&A Homes launched a similar promotion in August 2010. Home shoppers could Like the S&A Homes page on Facebook and download a coupon for $1,500 toward the purchase of options. The coupon and the Facebook page launched at approximately the same time to create a buzz. Six buyers downloaded and redeemed the coupons.

Figure 5.1 Highland Homes Facebook page

Highland Homes posts and interacts daily with prospects and agents on its Facebook page.

Source: Reprinted with permission from Highland Homes, Lakeland, Florida

In addition, some S&A Homes buyers have liked the builder's page after signing a contract. This facilitates buyers referring their friends to the builder through social media.

When S&A Homes launched its Facebook page (fig. 5.2), the company strategically targeted real estate agents to Like the page—and more than 100 did within

Figure 5.2 **S&A Homes' Facebook page**

S&A Homes promotes its incentives and specials on its Facebook page.

Source: Reprinted with permission from S&A Homes, State College, Pennsylvania

weeks. Again, the company offered an incentive—a $10 Sheetz gas card. To participate, agents simply had to Like the page and write on the wall. The campaign promoted S&A's blog, e-mail messages (fig. 5.3), and, of course, its Facebook page.

Comments posted on the wall included "Great quality and great people!" and "Sold 2 S&A Homes . . . easy to work with and both clients were very pleased."

Figure 5.3 Sheetz e-mail incentive

The Sheetz $10 gift card incentive encouraged Realtors to Like the S&A Homes Facebook page and write on its wall

S&A HOMES E-INCENTIVE FOR REALTORS!

S&A Homes hopes to put some "**drive**" back into the economy and a few lucky Realtors will be able to put some gas in their tanks. Our new E-Incentive offers the first 200 Realtors who"like" our S&A Homes corporate Facebook page a **$10 Sheetz gift card.**

E-Incentive Directions:
Realtors, if you want to receive a $10 Sheetz gift card, here are the steps:

1. Log into your Facebook account
2. "Like" the S&A Homes' corporate page @ www.facebook.com/sahomes
3. Post one thing you love about S&A Homes.

After you have signed up and posted a message, a representative will contact you directly to mail your gift card.

   www.facebook.com/sahomes

www.sahomesblog.com

Source: Reprinted with permission from S&A Homes, State College, Pennsylvania

Wall posters even complimented specific employees on their customer service.

Twitter

Twitter is a *microblog* that allows users to, essentially, send text messages or instant messages (IMs) to the world. Twitter users send and receive *tweets* (messages) of no more than 140 characters. Your followers can log on to http://www.Twitter.com to see your *stream* of tweets. People will decide whether they want to follow you or not based your profile and the content of your tweets. If all of your tweets are push marketing–your events, your homes, your stuff–your audience will lose interest quickly. Consider your frustration with e-mail spam like "Be number one on Google," "Join my multilevel marketing program," "Buy this great drug without a prescription from Canada." Now folks are bombarded with these same messages on Twitter, so don't add to the spam.

You may want to set up multiple accounts on Twitter. You could have a company account for your remodeling, building, or brokerage company, and an account for you as an individual. Carefully think through how you will set up these accounts before building them. Each company has a unique marketing culture. If you create a corporate account, you should include the Twitter bio of whoever is tweeting for the company. Go to http://Twitter.com/

montehewett, http://Twitter.com/GerstadBuilders, or http://Twitter.com/AstoriaCondos for some ideas about how to show who is tweeting for your company.

Setting Up a Twitter Account

Choose a name that will help users locate your company. Twitter allows 15 characters for your name. If you are Michael Robin, choose your name rather than MR846, so people can find you.

- Complete your profile.
- Name
- Location (your city and state)
- Website URL
- Bio—your background and what you do or information about the person tweeting for the account
- Your photo or company logo

People will choose to follow you and your company based on your profile and your tweets. They may not think you are a real person if your profile is incomplete or you have never tweeted.

Twitter Terminology

Direct messages. It is easy to send a personal message to another twitter user by choosing Messages from the top navigation area. Click a follower's name on the drop-down menu on the left of the screen, or click New Message and enter the contact's name in the designated space. This will send the tweet directly to another Twitter user, similar to an e-mail message.

Hash tag. The pound sign (#); provides a method to categorize tweets, search for specific subjects, and track trends. Twitter can now be searched without using the hash tag, but many people still use it to organize content.

Retweet (RT). Sending a tweet from another user; similar to forwarding an e-mail message.

Tweet. A message posted on Twitter.

User name. The name under which an individual's or company's tweets will appear, such as @AtlantaPR. The corresponding Twitter URL is http://Twitter.com/AtlantaPR.

Tweeting With Personality

You have only 140 characters to make an impact, so make your tweets fun. What you say doesn't have to be personal, but it should have personality. Reserve about 30 characters of your tweet so readers who Like it can easily comment on and retweet it. This means that you really only have about 110 characters per tweet. You can

- tweet about your business;
- provide tips (seasonal home care, best remodeling projects, landscaping ideas);

- share news (tax credits, mortgage rates, incentives);
- retweet other content; and
- ask questions and engage in conversations.

Vary your message. No more than 25% of your tweets should be about yourself or your company. Aim for a ratio of between 12:1 and 3:1 of tweets about yourself or your company to other tweets. Include URLs, photos, and videos, and link to your website or blog.

You must shorten long URLs to save space when tweeting. Many Twitter applications already do this, but if you are tweeting directly on Twitter, you can use http://www.TinyURL.com or www.Bitly.com.

Here are some good Tweets from home builders I follow. They demonstrate a mix of promotion and engagement. Make sure that you are having conversations on Twitter and not just promoting your products and services.

@BooneHomes

Want to save 38.1% on your energy bill? Our Richmond new homes with EnergyStar features can help http://bit.ly/gXeEGM

@BooneHomes

Sweet!! Spring is almost here! Time to paint that used home ... unless you live in a Boone Homes No maintenance community.

@AKRenovations

Doing housework? Don't you wish you had this adorable helper? http://bit.ly/hdrYnK

@LancasterHomes

RT @aftanfisher: This is my house!! Thanks @Lancasterhomes http://yfrog.com/hs5ltypj

@abqbuilder

If home is where the heart is, why would you want to go with the cheapest bidder?

@LennarAtlanta

We just hit over 9,000 upload views on our youtube channel. Want to help us reach 10,000? http://bit.ly/9FHqjo

@LennarAtlanta

Confirmed @Reformationbrew will be providing some of their new product for tasting at #OTPtweetup be among the 1st! http://bit.ly/g8bkaI

Following People

If you're already on Twitter, are you following customers who will buy from you? Or are you only following people in the industry? Even worse, do you automatically follow everyone who follows you? If so, most of your "followers" are probably *bots* (robots that automate Internet tasks) or spammers. You must follow the right people on Twitter.

The right people are consumers who either will buy from you or influence someone else to buy from you. How do you find the right people? Sometimes finding one person and reviewing their list of followers will help you to find 10 more followers (birds of a feather flock together). Home builders will probably want to follow real estate agents and remodelers may want to start by following their best referral sources. Develop the strategy that you think will work best for your company and then review its effectiveness after 30, 60, and 90 days.

Searching for Followers

Review the followers of your influencers. These may be real estate agents, vendors, or just friends. Observe who your target market is following, including competitors.

- Use the People Search function on Twitter. (You must know exactly who you are looking for.).
- Search for profile types using the advanced search on Twitter.
- Search Twellow (http://www.twellow.com) for related profiles.
- Use Tweepz (http://www.tweepz.com) to find matching profiles.

Participating in online events that use hash tags will also increase your followers. For example, I sometimes participate in #blogchat and #linkedinchat. Twitter chats provide an opportunity to meet new people with similar interests from around the country, while sharing expertise.

Once you have followers you'll want to build lists. If you are following 500 or 1,000 people it can be hard to keep up with all the tweets you want to read because the Twitter stream moves so rapidly. One way to see more of what you want to read is by building lists to isolate specific groups. Each list can contain up to 500 Twitter accounts and you can create up to 20 lists. You can include users you are not following in your lists to keep up with their tweets. For example you can build lists for real estate agents, suppliers, and competitors. This allows you sort tweets. Consider locking your lists if you don't want to share that great group of city-specific agents you've spent time building.

Customize Your Twitter Background

Twitter is a branding opportunity for your company. Even if you choose a basic background, use your corporate colors. If you don't know the numbered code (*hexadecimal code*) for the colors, you can get them from your website designer so you can match the colors precisely. If you want to go further with your brand, hire a graphic artist to create a custom background for your Twitter page. Consider placing important information about your company, such as your website URL and phone number, on the left side of your template so people who visit your page can easily contact you by phone or find your website.

For more tips on customizing your Twitter background, consult http://mashable.com/2009/05/23/ Twitter-backgrounds/or Google (search "free Twitter backgrounds").

Twitter Do's

- Choose a name that makes sense.
- Complete your entire profile.
- Follow the people that you want to follow you.
- Retweet others' interesting tweets.
- Ask questions and engage in conversation.
- Start slowly by following a number of accounts and spend time just reading and listening.
- Twitter is a tool for immediate conversation, not what happened 12 hours ago. Respond to "@" replies and direct messages as you receive them.
- Build lists of followers to allow you to break through the clutter and focus on specific groups.

Twitter Don'ts

- Read every message that your followers post; you will never catch up.
- Use Twitter for blatant self promotion. Instead, share useful information, build a relationship, converse.
- Forget that when you write something online, it lasts forever. If you wouldn't say it in real life (IRL), don't tweet it.
- Tweet about mundane events (we don't care what you ate for breakfast).
- Lash out if you are attacked by a follower. Instead think about the appropriate response and when you do respond, be transparent and honest.
- Engage *trolls*. Trolls post off-topic messages that are usually hurtful, controversial, or inflammatory on Twitter, Facebook, blogs, or other social sites.

Twitter Applications

Applications help organize your life on Twitter. They have built-in URL shortening, allow users to create groups of followers, sort through numerous tweets quickly, and enable you to manage multiple accounts from one location.

Twitter apps for smartphones make it easy to tweet on the go. If you don't yet have a smartphone, you can still text tweets from a cell phone. Integrating Twitter into your daily routine makes it less of an interruption and something you are more likely to keep up with. I may check tweets on my iPhone while cleaning stalls in my barn or on the way to dinner (with someone else driving of course!).

For PC or Mac, try Tweet Deck, HootSuite, or Seesmic or Social Oomph. For smartphones, try HootSuite, TwitterBerry, Tweetie, Tweet Deck.

Twitter Searches

Monitor Twitter conversations. You need to know what others are saying about you and your brand. Here are some quick and easy ways to do this:

- Search any company name or phrase to find out what's currently on Twitter by using either http://search.Twitter.com or http://twendz.waggeneredstrom.com.
- From your Twitter home page, check to see who is mentioning you by clicking on @Mentions in the navigation choices under What's happening. You will see Timeline, @Mentions, Retweets, Searches, and Lists. Monitor these tweets carefully because they could be questions about your business.

- Create automated searches using your Twitter app (like Tweet Deck). At a minimum, create these for your company's name and your name.
- Use Google Alerts http://www.google.com/alerts (a free service) to set up alerts for your name, your company, and even your competitors.

Promote your Twitter Account

Promote your Twitter account as you do your Facebook page. List your Twitter account on your website, blog, e-mail signature, Facebook page, and other communications using the Twitter icon or a link in your text. To maximize the effectiveness of Twitter, invest time to find followers, post content, and engage in conversation.

Gathering a Crowd with Twitter

Los Angeles marketing and public relations firm red rocket LA turned West Los Angeles loft residences into a destination, thanks to Twitter. TLofts (fig. 5.4), an eco-friendly loft community in Los Angeles, Calif., was completely new to social media but embraced the idea to attract its target market of hip young professionals.

Despite its location on a busy thoroughfare amid more than 2 million sq. ft. of office space, the building's sales team was not reaching the 7,000 professionals who

Figure 5.4 **TLofts on Twitter**

TLofts used Twitter to communicate food truck news, draw foot traffic, and create a community for ongoing conversations.

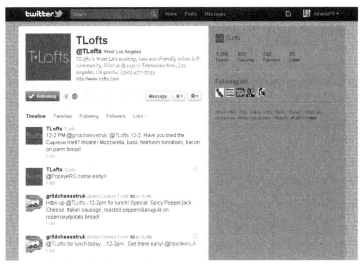

Source: Reprinted with permission from Red Rocket LA, Culver City, California

worked there. Meanwhile, a gourmet food street truck phenomenon had recently emerged on L.A.'s young professional scene. Kogi Korean BBQ was hot, with hundreds of customers every night, and the only way to find out where the truck would be on a given evening was to follow the restaurant on Twitter or visit its website.

TLofts' social media team joined forces with Kogi by having the truck visit its sales center during the day (at lunchtime and at other times of the day when nobody normally would be able to get their hands on a coveted Kogi taco). TLoft and Kogi both tweeted about the truck's midday stop at the TLofts' sales center, and more than 50 customers were waiting outside the sales center for the truck before it arrived. The line grew to 100 people, many of whom were tweeting, texting, and e-mailing their friends and colleagues about the truck's stop at TLofts. Soon, other gourmet food street trucks wanted to park outside the TLofts sales center, so the team hosted a different street truck every day for 10 days. Now TLofts and large hungry crowds welcome the Kogi truck each week. As a result, TLofts gained visibility and more sales center traffic. The building opened in mid-August 2009 and in early 2011 only 6 lofts were left.

Since its initial success with the Kogi BBQ Truck, the social media team has continued to connect with groups on Twitter that match its target demographics, including restaurants, bars, shops, and individuals following those establishments. The success of the Kogi Korean BBQ truck attracted other food truck operators who heard the buzz via Twitter and word-of-mouth. They started asking to park at the community for lunch as well. Soon, TLofts had more than 20 trucks jockeying for time slots and a different truck started coming to the site every day, including the Grilled Cheese Truck, Joe Kabob, India Jones (Indian food), Sprinkles Cupcake truck, Nom Nom Truck (Vietnamese food), and Buttermilk Truck (breakfast food). So, while TLofts tweets one to five times daily, the trucks, which all use Twitter extensively, are also tweeting about TLofts every day. Talk about viral marketing!

The connections TLofts made through its social marketing efforts also helped the company demonstrate leadership as a corporate citizen. After the earthquake in Haiti, TLofts asked the food trucks to participate in a fund-raiser to benefit the survivors. Days after the earthquake, 26 trucks gathered at Tlofts and promised to donate part or all of their profits for onc day to the Red Cross for Haiti earthquake relief. More than 5,000 people attended the fund-raiser in response to tweets about the event. The food truck partnership raised $7,000 for Haitian earthquake relief. In addition, food, real estate, culture blogs, and two local TV stations covered the event.

YouTube

YouTube is a video sharing network with user profiles and channels. Consumers can view homes, communities, and projects on it, and take virtual tours. You can use it to teach about an aspect of remodeling, show off a Parade of Homes project, or help a client view a specific room or home feature from a remote location. Just record a video and upload it YouTube. You can make the video private or public.

You can store videos for all of your websites on YouTube. Load videos on YouTube and link to them from your blog, website, Facebook page, Twitter account, and other locations. Search engines love video, so an account on YouTube will boost your SEO and ranking in the SERPs.

Setting Up the Account

Go to http://www.youtube.com and click "Create Account" in the top right corner of the home page. Complete the entire profile, including a description and website URL. Your username will be part of your YouTube URL. For example, the username "JohnDoe" would result in a profile URL of http://www.youtube.com/user/johndoe. If you need technical help, visit http://www.Google.com/support/youtube/.

Customize your channel:

- Enter a channel title. You can use spaces between words.
- Add channel tags. Include your company name and other keywords.
- Add themes and colors. Choose from the standard options or use the advanced options to fully customize your channel.

Choose what to display, from comments to friends to recent activity in the modules. This is what others will see when they visit your channel.

Start Uploading

Now you can upload videos! Title each video and add a description and tags (YouTube's term for keywords) to help search engines find the video. In addition to posting videos, you can subscribe to other YouTube user profiles, join groups, and create lists of favorite videos. This will help increase your company's visibility on YouTube. When consumers visit other profiles and see your icon, they are likely to click through to see your videos and may subscribe to your content.

YouTube Tips

Viewers will share funny, entertaining, or informative videos with others.

- Keep videos short—90 seconds to 2 minutes.
- Use a Flip camera or your smartphone to capture videos. (You don't necessarily need a professional to shoot video, although you may want to hire a pro for certain projects.)
- Post virtual tours of your homes and remodeling projects.

- Post quick house tours privately for remote custom clients.
- Enlist homeowners to shoot videos for you.
- Observe how other companies use YouTube.

Helping Customers Visualize

Central Florida home builder Highland Homes first started shooting videos of homes three years ago to increase customer satisfaction. The company builds over a wide geographic region and wanted its customers to be able to see finished homes from plans that were not under construction in their local area. To help customers visualize the completed homes, a motivated agent recorded video tours of finished homes from each floor plan.

The videos made the sales presentation go much more smoothly because customers could view a high-definition video of a floor plan on the spot. It eliminated the need to give prospects a $25 gas card incentive to drive to models in remote locations.

Kathie McDaniel, Broker, MCSP, MIRM, and vice president of sales and marketing for Highland Homes says the company uses a professional videographer to record examples of all its floor plans as the homes are built to add to the builder's library (fig. 5.5). The company also has added videos of its Personal Selection Studio to its YouTube account. Buyers who view the clips prior to making selections are more prepared to make selections and they request fewer change orders than those who haven't viewed these videos, she says.

Trulia

Trulia is a free real estate search engine with embedded social networking tools for consumers. Home builders, remodelers, and real estate agents can use it to interact with buyers. If you are an agent or a broker, claim your listings on the site. Home builders, remodelers, and agents should take advantage of the site's free blog and Q&A section for home seekers. You can use the site to reach buyers directly and to promote your homes and neighborhoods more broadly.

Creating your Profile

- Go to http://www.Trulia.com and click Sign up.
- Complete the form and click Create Account.
- In the Quick Links box at the top right, select My Profile.
- Describe yourself in the headline (e.g., Jacksonville New Homes Specialist).
- Add your website URL, blog, and links to your other social media sites.

Figure 5.5 Highland Homes YouTube channel

Highland Homes created a library of videos that allows people to take virtual home tours and select options.

- Set the URL for your public profile (e.g., http://www.Trulia.com/profile/carolflammer/).
- Complete the sections on Experience, About Me, and Testimonials.

In the Experience section you may want to list your past two to three positions or detail your credentials. Under About Me, discuss your specialties and provide some insight into your personality. Then find clients or customers to add testimonials to your page. If you already have testimonials that you have permission to use online, add them.

Claim your Listings

After creating your user profile, claim your listings. Click My Listings (you must be logged in) and find listings by property address, MLS ID, or e-mail address. By claiming listings, you will have access to edit your listings and can see how many times people have viewed them. This will provide you with information on how many times the listing is viewed. Listings are claimed on a "first-come, first-served" basis. The agent (or other profile user) that claims first gets their contact information on that listing, so make sure you get to your listings first!

Blogging on Trulia

You can post blogs and create links to your website and custom blog free on Trulia. It is simple to use, so it can be a great place to start blogging and build a following while your own blog is under construction. You can create referring links by using keywords and anchor text. Follow these steps:

- Click Write New Post to start a new post.
- Add a title (informative, catchy, and brief). Titles need to capture attention or you won't attract readers. Consider the newspaper headlines or evening news promotions that entice you to watch. My post titled "Where's My Homebuyer Tax Credit?" attracted 106 views without any promotion.
- Select a category.
- Add your location.
- Type a 250–350-word, conversational blog entry. Although you can cut and paste text, you must do it from a plain text program like Notepad that will not add unnecessary coding.
- Include a link or two in your text. Highlight the anchor text and click the link icon on the toolbar (fig. 5.6).
- Copy and paste the URL of the website or page you are linking to.

Figure 5.6 Blog on Trulia

Blogging on Trulia will increase exposure for your homes and communities to consumers.

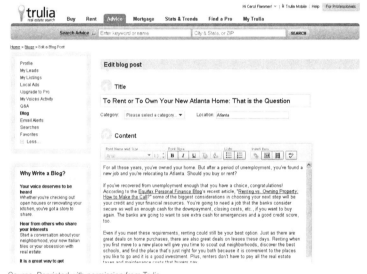

Source: Reprinted with permission from Trulia

- Enter a description of the website or page.
- Add at least one photo, sized appropriately for the web (72 *dpi* = medium resolution). Click the photo box in the toolbar and browse your computer or the Internet for the image. You can click More Options to specify where in the post you want the image to appear. You can also enter an image description.

- Click done.
- Click Publish.
- Review your blog entry and edit it, if necessary.

Q&A with Potential Buyers

You can establish expertise in a niche and create relationships with potential home buyers by answering questions on Trulia. Buyers ask questions on topics from how to repair their credit to how to buy a foreclosed property.

- Click Q&A in the My Trulia box at the upper right area of the page.
- Click the Trulia Voices link in the middle of the page.
- Click View Most Recent Questions to peruse them.
- To answer a question, click it. Then click, Answer This Question and type your answer.
- To ask a question, type it in the text box in the Ask a Question box.

ActiveRain

With more than 192,000 members, ActiveRain (http://www.activerain.com) promotes itself as the largest online gathering of real estate professionals in the world. The

ActiveRain Real Estate Network is free and provides opportunities for home builders, remodelers, real estate agents, and others in the real estate community to interact.

A basic profile is free, but becoming a Rainmaker offers exposure outside the ActiveRain network to search engines and to the more than 2 million monthly consumer visitors to the site. Rainmakers also can access training from industry-leading experts. ActiveRain can be a great way to add another result to your page one SERP results and interact with co-op agents who can help sell your homes.

Creating an Account

Select Login on the upper right corner of the home page and follow the directions. You will see a screen that allows you to log in or to sign up to create an account. As with YouTube, your username will be part of your URL on ActiveRain. For example, my username is CarolFlammer, so my profile URL is http://ActiveRain.com/carolflammer.

You will receive a confirmation e-mail message with a link. When you click the link, you can update your profile as follows:

- Upload a profile photo or company logo.
- Explain who you are and your specialty in the About Me section.

- Complete your profile with pertinent information that makes you stand out. You can customize and rename sections to make them more applicable to your company. You can add links to your website, Facebook page, Twitter profile, blog, and other sites.

After you are satisfied with your profile, start looking for associates (the equivalent of Facebook friends). You can also join the groups of other real estate professionals within specific niches of the real estate industry and ActiveRain.

ActiveRain also gives you a personal blog and the capability to send your blog posts to Localism.com (a consumer portal), your group members, categories, and other ActiveRain channels.

Using the Blog

Click Write a Blog Post at the top of the page to start a new post.

- Title your entry.
- Type your entry or cut and paste it from a text editor like Notepad.
- Add a link or two to your text by highlighting the word or words you want to link to and clicking the link icon on the toolbar.

- Enter the entire site address.
- Leave target as "Open link in a new window."
- Title the link.
- Select three to four relevant tags. (Include these words in your blog post.)
- Add photos. Click the box in the toolbar with the tree. If you click the box to the right of the image URL you can upload from your computer instead of entering a URL. Enter an image description and a title and use the appearance tab to specify where in the post the image will appear. Click insert.
- Select the channels, groups, and categories you wish to post to.
- Publish, review, and edit your entry as necessary.

Finding Associates

- Click Search at the top right of the page.
- Type keywords (e.g., "St. Paul," "golf communities").
- To narrow the search results to individuals only, click members at the top of the page.
- When you see a member you think you want to connect with, click their link and view their profile.

- From their profile, click Add as Associate under their profile picture and add them to a group.

You can also add notes about them. These will be visible to anyone viewing the associates on your profile.

Joining Groups

- Click Groups at the top right of the page, next to Search.
- You can search for groups in two ways:
- To view groups in various catcgorics, use the drop-down box under Browse Groups.
- Type a keyword in the text box under Search Groups and click Search.
- To join, click the group's link.
- On the left of the group page, click Join Group.

You can share your blog posts with a group by selecting it from the drop-down menu on your blog.

If you want to post a blog entry only to the group's profile, go to that group and click Post to Group at the top left of the page. Type your blog post as you normally would. This will publish your entry only in the group, not on your personal blog.

RealtyJoin

RealtyJoin (http://www.RealtyJoin.com) is a social networking site designed to help real estate investors, service providers, home builders, remodelers and other professionals find opportunities and establish connections. RealtyJoin users can create enhanced profiles. Each user has a personal WordPress blog on the site. The site also has options for loading videos, photos, seeking project bids online, and social networking.

Creating an Account

- Select the Sign Up Today button in the upper right corner of the site.
- Create an account by completing all of the profile details (what site visitors see) and all of the account details (information you will use to login). Click Create Account.
- Type your first and last name separated—for example, Carol Flammer—in the profile details.
- In the account details, combine your name and use all lowercase letters, for example "carolflammer." The next screen offers various levels of registration from free, to premium, to executive level. You may want to start with the free membership and upgrade it later.

- After you have joined the site, you can log in by entering your user name and password at the top right area of the page.
- If your profile photo does not automatically display, go to Gravatar (http://www.gravatar.com) and get a globally recognized avatar. Your Gravatar is associated with your e-mail address so wherever you log in with that address your Gravatar will be displayed.
- Click My Account at the top right of the page. You will see a personal dashboard with friend requests, group activity, and messages. You can edit your profile there.
- Add a logo to your profile. I resized the mRELEVANCE logo to 400 pixels wide to get it to display properly on my profile.

RealtyJoin also gives you a personal WordPress blog but you must set it up. Click the Express Yourself: Start Your Own RealtyJoin Blog button on the right side of your profile page.

Create your blog as follows:

- Name your blog. It will display in the masthead at the top of your blog, so use proper capitalization and spaces between words.
- Create your blog's URL, for example, http://realtyjoin.com/carolflammer.

- Choose the desired privacy level. There are two options. I recommend the first one, which is to allow your blog to be visible in the search engines. The second option will only display your blog posts to others on the RealtyJoin site.

Using the Blog

You can customize the blog header. Review the appearance options in the drop-down menu.

Edit the About page. Write a short autobiography or an overview of your blog and what you plan to write about. This will help readers determine whether they want to follow you.

Once you are ready to blog, go to the Dashboard and click Add New from the Posts drop-down menu on the left side of the dashboard.

If you don't want to use HTML code, use the Visual Editor.

- Type the title of your post under Add New Post.
- Type your entry or cut and paste it from a text editor like Notepad.
- Add a link or two to your text by highlighting the word or words you want to link to and clicking the link icon on the toolbar.
- Enter the link address.

- Leave target as "Open link in a new window."
- Title the link.
- Select three to four relevant tags. These words also should be included in your blog entry.
- Select a category for your post. You will need to add categories the first time you post.
- Add photos. Click the box to the right of upload/ insert. If you have trouble uploading, you may want to select the browser uploader option. There are also options to upload from an URL or a media library.
- Preview your entry, edit it, and click Publish when you are ready to post it live.

Connecting with RealtyJoin Members

RealtyJoin offers many options for connecting to others:

- Use the search box at the top right of the site to search for a specific member by name.
- Click on "Member Profile" from the top navigation to review RealtyJoin members and select ones you want to connect with for business.
- Use the "Invite Anyone" option in the left sidebar to invite contacts that would benefit from the site.

Joining Groups

Click Groups in the top navigation. You can review groups and choose an existing group to join. You can start your own group by selecting "create a group."

Linkedin

Linked in is an online Rolodex and résumé. Use it to

- build connections;
- cstablish expertise by asking and answering questions
- gain recommendations; and
- post jobs and events.

Linkedin is a great tool for building personal brand. You can create a page for your business as well. The search engines index both personal and business pages. After building your Linkedin account, promote it via your website, blog, e-mail signature, Facebook page, and your other sites.

Linkedin helps you maintain contact with people no matter how many times they change jobs. I use it as a mini *customer relationship management* (*CRM*) system for my connections. Linkedin allows me to keep up with people that I don't need to e-mail every day so I don't overwhelm my Outlook contacts database. I try to invite everyone I meet to connect with me via Linked in, so I can reach out to them in the future when the right opportunity arises.

Creating an Account

Create your public profile. Think executive bio.

- Name (women might want to include their maiden name)
- Former employers or companies (former associ- ates may not know where you are now)
- Photo
- Education
- Contact information (phone number & e-mail)
- URL (website, blog, other sites you own)
- Twitter (add your Twitter account, but don't set it to post everything you tweet to your Linkedin account)
- Customize your public profile's URL.
- Choose what to include in your public profile.

Making Connections

After setting up your account, connect with people.

- Send a personal note with your invitation.
- Connect with colleagues. Linkedin can search your e-mail for connections or you can add people you find using Linkedin's search function.

- Clean out that drawer or box of business cards you have and add these contacts to Linkedin. You can finally throw the cards away!
- Add new people you meet to your Linkedin account.
- Ask your connections to introduce you to their connections on Linkedin using the Get Introduced function.

Having lots of connections increases the likelihood that people will see your profile first, even if they're searching for someone else.

Managing Your Connections

You can manage your connections by making notes on your connections profiles (these notes are only visible to you). If you need to look up a person whose name you can't remember, you can sort contacts by state or industry. If you need more robust management tools, consider upgrading to a paid account.

Recommendations

Request recommendations from your best customers and provide recommendations for your vendors. Providing recommendations positions your name on the person's page you are recommending and increases your visibility. For example, if you love this book, please go to my Linkedin profile (http://www.linkedin.com/in/carol flammer) and add a recommendation. You can do the same for your framer, real estate agent, plumber, sign company, and others you work with. If you like their work, tell them and other people.

Create a Company Profile

Linkedin company profiles display the date the company was founded, a corporate biography, number of employees, and the average age of the employees. Clients and associates can review your company's profiles prior to meeting you for useful background and corporate culture information prior to business meetings. Also add the following:

- Company name
- Logo
- Biography
- Specialties
- Related companies
- Your blog

Make sure employees list the company name correctly on their profiles so they will appear on Linkedin's roster for your company.

Posting and Finding Jobs

The jobs section of Linkedin allows you to post available jobs at your company and to research available jobs with other companies. This is a great way to find qualified employees as well as your next job. The Find Jobs section automatically populates with jobs that match your current job description. You also can search for jobs by job title, keywords, or company name. Posting a job is easy, but not free.

Events

You can post and join events on Linkedin. This is a good tool to promote webinars, classes, and other special events to your connections. Find or create new events by clicking the More tab in the main navigation and selecting Events from the drop-down menu. Your Events home page will display all the events created by your connections. To find an event, click the Find Events tab and search by city or location and keywords. Click Add an Event to create your own event. After you create an event, you can invite contacts using InMail. Home builders frequently use LinkedIn to invite real estate agents to luncheons or open houses. If you host parties for homeowners, you could invite them through LinkedIn as well.

Groups

You can position yourself as an expert by joining or starting groups on Linkedin and become a connector. Groups are a great way to field questions, share news stories and interact with others. The number of groups on Linkedin can be overwhelming, so start with groups that you are already a member of IRL. NAHB has a group, as does the 50+ Housing Council, Professional Women in Building, and the National Sales and Marketing Council (NSMC). These online groups allow you to sustain and extend your relationships with members beyond monthly or quarterly meetings. Linkedin also suggests groups you may like based on your profile. Visit some of them to see if you want to participate in them.

Linkedin Do's

- Secure your URL.
- Complete your entire profile.
- Update you status weekly.
- Join groups.
- Write recommendations.
- Create a corporate profile.
- Answer questions—the more you give the more you get back.

Linkedin Don'ts

- Feel pressured to give an introduction or recommendation.
- Forward questionable requests to your connections.
- Become spam by inviting everyone you remotely know to connect.
- Forget to update your status at least once a month.

Why to Use Linkedin

- Increase your visibility and build personal brand.
- Make connections and build a better network.
- Improve your Google results.
- Perform reference checks on individuals and companies.
- Gauge the health of a company.
- Ask for advice.
- Give advice and establish your expertise.

Tying it Together With Online Apps

Linkedin offers a number of applications to tie your social media sites together. Review them and incorporate some into your profile.

- Blog (WordPress or TypePad). Incorporate your WordPress or TypePad blog into your Linkedin personal profile.
- Company Buzz. Add tweets about your company or other key search terms to your profile.
- SlideShare and Google Presentation. Make your latest presentations available online.
- Box.net. Share and collaborate on an array of file types.
- MyTravel. Allow others to see your travel schedule using TripIt.
- Reading List by Amazon. Share what you are reading with others.
- Polls. Find out what your connections think about a specific topic by adding a poll to your profile.
- Huddle Workspaces. Collaborate on a project with others in a private workspace.

Joining Groups Keeps Those Far Away Closer

The NAHB's Professional Women in Building Network has a group on Linkedin (fig 5.7). We use it to keep in touch with one another between board meetings and to promote the council's events. We have discussed best practices for social media and how to motivate staff during tough economic times. A recent post promoted a scholarship awards webinar and explained how to participate in the awards. Group members have used the Get Introduced feature to create a warm handshake in today's competitive business environment.

Figure 5.7 Professional Women in Building Linkedin group page

Professional Women in Building stay connected and share ideas through a LinkedIn group.

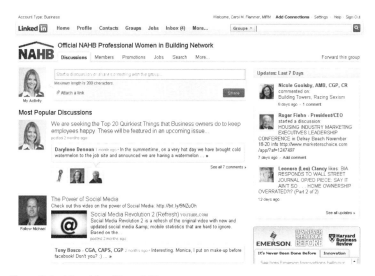

Source: National Association of Home Builders

Photo Sharing Sites

A study by BHI Media[34] on home elevations revealed that color renderings or photos on home listings and on the builder's website increased the number of home shoppers who click for more details by 30%. On the other hand, a line drawing, black and white photo, or no image decreased clicks by 30%. Take advantage of the web to show off your homes and communities in full color.

Flickr

Flickr allows users to load and share galleries of photos along with their profiles. Because Yahoo! owns Flickr, it ranks high in a Yahoo! image search. When you post photos on Flickr you increase the likelihood that they will appear in the results when users enter your keywords in their photo searches. Pictures are a valuable marketing asset. Make sure they are professional. Because Flickr is for non-commercial use, you must not use the site to sell through your captions and descriptions.

To increase the likelihood that search engines will find your photos, tag and title them appropriately. Instead of naming your photo "Chestnut Crossing," consider labeling it with more keywords. For example: "Chestnut Crossing Single Family Homes [Name of Builder]

Georgetown KY 38888." You could include even more descriptors, such as three-bedroom home, energy efficient, or anything else home buyers might be seeking that your home and community provide. Remodelers should post before and after photos of kitchen, master bedroom, and bathroom projects with keywords that homeowners might use when searching for a remodeling company.

Creating an Account

Click Create Your Account on the home page and enter your Yahoo ID. (To get a Yahoo ID, go to Yahoo.com and click Sign Up. This ID will allow you to create a My Yahoo page and use tools in addition to Flickr, such as Yahoo instant messaging and Yahoo Mail.)

Personalize your profile.

- Create your "buddy icon" by uploading your logo or photo.
- Choose your customized Flickr URL (your company name or your name according to whether the page is for personal or business use. Mine is http://www.flickr.com/photos/mrelevance).
- Personalize your profile with your name, time zone, gender, and description. (If you are creating a business profile, just add the time zone and description.)
- Upload photos.

- Add tags (keywords) and descriptions.
- Create sets (photo groupings). You may want to create a set of photos for a specific community or group photos by floor plan or room type.
- Find friends on Flickr. Search an existing address book on Yahoo, Gmail, or Windows live.
- Search for people by name. You can add a person to your account as a contact, friend, or family member.
- Join groups. Find groups on Flickr that match your interests. Groups exist for green building, condos, home and garden, and other industry specialties.

Photo sharing websites add another dimension to your social networking through Facebook and Twitter, and enable you to post photos easily to your blog and on other sites. As with YouTube, a photo sharing site can help you show images of a home under construction to clients without having them go to the jobsite.

Making a Visual Impression

Atlanta, Georgia, kitchen and bath supplier, Construction Resources Inc. uses Flickr to showcase its products in finished installations (fig. 5.8). This has been a great way to reach out to consumers, architects and designers.

Figure 5.8 **A Flickr page**

A robust photo gallery can help buyers visualize your products.

Source: Reprinted with permission from Construction Resources, Decatur, Georgia.

"We showcase our products as well as our events on the site," said Mitch Hires, president of Construction Resources. "This provides a very compelling visual example of our available products and our finished work. Because homeowners have a hard time visualizing what the final installation of their countertop or other products might look like, our photos on Flickr give them an opportunity to visualize the possibilities."

Tampa, Florida, REALTOR®, Richard Nappi, CSP, of The Nappi Group, bought an inexpensive digital camera four years ago and began using Flickr on a whim. "I wasn't sure exactly what I was doing, but just thought I'd try it out." Now he has more than 8,000 photos of homes in and around the Tampa area in his Flickr account. New clients have found him through his photos. "Home buyers want pictures, pictures, and more pictures," Nappi says. To answer this demand, he includes a Flickr slideshow of select homes in his follow-up e-mails. He also posts these slide-shows on YouTube and posts photos on his website and other photo sharing sites.

Other Internet Tools

The Internet offers hundreds, if not thousands, of other so-cial networking sites, coupon sites, and tools to consider:

- Craigslist (http://www.craigslist.org) advertises jobs, housing, items for sale, personals, events, and more, for free. Consider listing homes, an-nouncing events, and posting press releases there. Builders and agents have reported great traffic from this site.
- Squidoo (http://www.squidoo.com) allows users to create free web pages (called lenses) on particu-lar topics or subjects. Consider launching a lens about your company and joining related groups.

- Ning (http://www.ning.com) allows users to create their own social networks around specific subject matter. Because great groups on homes and real estate already exist, you don't need to create your own. Just join and participate in an existing Ning group for your target market.

- New Homes Section (http://www.newhomes section.com) is an industry-specific listing service and blog. Consider e-mailing press releases to be included on the site.

- Foursquare (http://www.foursquare.com) offers users the opportunity to create local content on their favorite places to shop, dine, and hang out in an interactive game. Check into a particular venue (such as your office, a restaurant, or the grocery store) more than anyone else and become "the mayor." Home builders can use Foursquare as a place to offer upgrades and incentives to users who check in. For example, you could offer $1,500 in upgrades, a free refrigerator, or a microwave for checking in at a particular community.

- Yelp (http://www.yelp.com) allows users to write reviews and recommendations of businesses including restaurants, stores, and nightclubs. Ask happy homeowners to contribute a positive review of your company here.

- Posterous (http://www.posterous.com) is a free service that will create a website and post content that you e-mail. If you want a blog but don't want to build and maintain it, you can e-mail your blog posts to Posterous. You can blog from your mobile phone. Although I prefer to use WordPress so I can control my blog, I use Posterous too (http://carolflammer.posterous.com/). I just don't update my Posterous blog as often.

- Google Profiles (http://www.Google.com/profiles/me) displays the results you want people to see when they Google your name. When you create your profile, you can include links to your website and social networking sites, and import photos from Flickr or other photo sharing sites.

- Social bookmarking sites enable users to share and manage articles and favorite websites. Yahoo Buzz, DIGG, Delicious, Propeller, Reddit, Sphinn, and Stumbleupon are some of my favorite bookmarking sites. By bookmarking content and adding tags, you can find web pages and websites easily in the future. For instance, while compiling statistics for this book, I bookmarked the statistics in my Delicious account (http://www.delicious.com/carolmflammer) and then tagged them "social media" and "statistics" or "women" and "statistics."

Later, I could sort by one of the tags to find all of the content related to that topic.

Text messaging can provide your buyers with instant gratification. When you include texting options on signs and ads, buyers can text you for information on your neighborhood, listing, or upcoming event. Sixty-eight percent of cell phone users[35] regularly send text messages. According to a survey conducted for Placecast by Harris Interactive,[36] many mobile users would like to receive alerts and information on their cell phones from places they frequent. A recent Harris Interactive survey[37] found that 42% of 18–34-year-olds and 33% of 35–44-year-olds with cell phones were interested in receiving alerts on their cell phones from places they frequent.

A quick response (QR) code, a two-dimensional bar code you scan using a smartphone with a QR code reader enables quick access to websites that display information contained in the QR code. (Scan the QR code on the back cover of this book for an example.) QR codes have several advantages: They can hold hundreds of times more information than traditional bar codes; they are readable from any direction; and even if they are slightly damaged or obscured, they are still readable. Real estate agents are using QR codes on signs and fly-ers to provide buyers with information, including videos of homes.

Build Systematically

Don't be overwhelmed by all the possible tools in your social media toolbox. Remember to start your SMM program with your blog as the hub. It will serve as the foundation of your entire program and can feed stories to a number of these social networking sites. Plan your program strategically to use the social networking sites that make the most sense to reach your target audiences. Smaller companies may want to choose to just use a blog and one or two social networking sites, whereas larger ones may want to launch and utilize most of the sites mentioned in this chapter. Social media is not one-size-fits-all. Just as you include the right home features for an individual buyer, you incorporate the right social media mix for your company.

Cost and Management of Social Media

f it's free why should I pay? Because "there's no such thing as a free lunch" definitely applies to the Internet. Social media programs require a significant investment of time and, usually, money.

However, building your marketing budget around a sound social media program and strategy will cost a fraction of what you previously spent on advertising. Work with a social media agency or consultant to create your strategy, build your sites, and tie everything together. A knowledgeable agency or consultant can coach your team along the way—explaining each site and best practices for social media optimization. By working with someone who has built multiple sites and already experienced the learning curve, you will save money and increase your program's effectiveness. Expect to spend $3,000 to $5,000 to set up your sites, including a self-hosted WordPress blog that you own, and $1,000–$5,000 per month (or more depending on factors such as the scope of your program and how many communities you are building in or managing) to maintain the sites and implement programs.

Why Can't My Niece Build My Facebook Page?

You wouldn't hire a trade with little or no experience to frame, roof, or finish a home to sell. Likewise, social media marketing and social networking demand professional expertise. Having your niece build one or two social networking sites without anyone in your company working with her to find the right friends, fans, and followers will not increase traffic or conversations to help you build your business. Launching a program with a poorly built blog, or no blog at all, will make social media optimization daunting. Make sure that the person or team you choose to build your SMM program thinks, plans, and mobilizes strategically. You will be even farther ahead of your competition if you work with a team with a social media track record.

Through the World Wide Web, you can either create fabulous curb appeal for your company or drive potential buyers away with a virtual front door that opens up to a confusing plan or no design at all. Remember, like any marketing effort, SMM should be strategic, have measurable goals, and complement your overall marketing and branding efforts.

Managing Social Media

Consider who will manage your social networking strategy. The marketing director? Sales manager? Online sales counselor? Receptionist? Agents? An outside agency? You can enlist a combination of team members. Your company's size will determine the answer, but a blend of internal and external management works well for most home builders. No matter who manages the strategy, you need one person to lead and direct it. Often, the sales agents, online sales counselor, or marketing director can take the lead answering questions and engaging agents and potential home buyers on social networking sites. Meanwhile, behind the scenes, a consultant or social media marketing company facilitates the team and either builds the sites or oversees site setup and trains the internal team to use sites.

Outsourcing

Look at many types of companies because every agency has unique capabilities. Do you need a firm to teach you how to converse with customers online in a meaningful way? Are you interested in driving traffic to your blog and website through SMO? Do you want to maintain a crisp brand image and promise online? Avoid making a costly mistake by understanding the necessary skills to build an effective social media program.

Following are eight critical questions to consider in evaluating the competency of a social media marketing consultant, agency, or team.

1. Do they have a blog? If companies or consultants are to build an effective blog for your company, they need to have built and run them successfully for themselves. Most seasoned social media marketers who can prove ROI understand how to build your program with the blog as the engine. An experienced consultant will have been blogging and building blogs since 2006 or 2007.

2. When you Google the company or consultant's name, what do you find? A seasoned social media marketer should have pages of search results mentioning the company name and personal name. How can you trust your online reputation to a company if it has not created a positive reputation of its own?

3. What social networking sites does the company or consultant use? If they believe in social media, they should be active on sites including Twitter, Facebook, Linkedin, Trulia, ActiveRain, YouTube, GoogleProfiles, and many others. They will have a portfolio reflecting many years of contributing to these sites.

4. What is the suggested strategy for using social media to achieve your overall marketing objectives? A competent social media marketer can build a strat-

egy that works for your team. Social media marketing is not one size fits all. Your goals will probably vary greatly even from those of your closest competitors. Your strategy should be part of an overall marketing plan.

5. What training will the company or consultant offer to you and your team? They should be able to train your team to use various sites and tools with training materials they have developed. They should be able to answer your questions or know where to find the answers.

6. Does the company or consultant understand SEO? Social media success is measured by traffic to your blog and website, and your ability to capture leads. Without SEO, you won't maximize these three areas. What is the web presence of the company or consultant you are considering hiring? Glancing at the title tags on their website, blog, or both, will tell you.

7. Can the company show you examples of its clients with netweaving? The ability to interconnect all of your sites increases their effectiveness exponentially. Ask for examples of clients with netweaved social media sites.

8. What return will you get from your investment in hiring the company or consultant? Will they provide reports, or at least advice on what to measure? How will they know what is working and what isn't?

Effective social media and search engine marketing starts with strategy and drives through implementation. You would not trust your brand identity and the *Four Ps* of marketing to someone new to your industry, so why would you trust your online brand image to someone without a proven online history and track record? Understanding product, price, place, promotion, and a fifth P—people—is critical to success in social media marketing.

Time Commitment

Most medium and large builders identify a team member to devote about 20 hours a week to blogging, posting, and conversing with potential clients. Of course, your strategy could include more or less time. Posting to your blog typically accounts for half of the time needed.

"Team blogging works well when you have a strong lead blogger. The lead blogger writes most of the blog content and other team members contribute ideas and post occasionally. One person must be responsible for the blog," says David L. Owen, president Boone Homes, Inc.

Choosing Sites and Developing Content

Your social media strategy could incorporate three sites or 30. After you have set goals and a budget for your program, you can determine how many sites to target. The basic sites for any successful campaign are a self-hosted WordPress blog, Facebook, YouTube, and Twitter. Following are three examples of what a program might encompass, based on builder size and market(s):

Small-Volume Builder

Blog. Post stories on your blog twice a week. Make sure to invite other members of your team to contribute information such as the following:

- **Community information.** Focus on your specific neighborhood or the greater area. If your neighborhood is next to the most popular ice cream store in the area, mention it. Don't forget community amenities and nearby shopping and restaurants. Isn't that new sushi restaurant down the street great?
- **Home plans.** Mention interesting features such as second-floor laundry rooms, 2.5-car garages, docking stations, large pantries, spa bathrooms, and flex space. Write your post so readers can feel what it is like to live in one of your homes ("You'll enjoy having a cup of coffee on the back deck overlooking the adjacent golf course.").
- **Home maintenance tips.** Provide advice on cleaning the gutters, caulking a tub, having the

HVAC serviced, cleaning the clothes dryer vent, and recognizing signs of insect infestation. You could provide a maintenance list for each season, or discuss how to tackle one chore on the list step-by-step.

- **Mortgage information and trends or other housing information.** Buying a home can be confusing, even if you have previously purchased one. Help your buyers to feel more comfortable with the process by telling them what to expect. Review the steps for a loan application, tell buyers how to get a copy of their credit score, and explain different types of loans.
- **Low-maintenance living.** Every builder has a slightly different interpretation of what low-maintenance living is. Therefore, define it—from exterior lawn care to painting and pressure washing the exterior, to snow removal.

Facebook. Update your Facebook status at least once or twice a week. Have your sales manager congratulate agents on recent sales and announce activities and events in your communities on Facebook. Include photos and albums of communities, homes, and events

Twitter. Follow all the agents you can find in your area and interact with them. Tweet thanks to them for bringing in home buyers, retweet their interesting posts and comment on their posts. Then expand your interaction to local restaurants and boutiques. Nobody wants to talk to themselves on Twitter. After you form relationships, converse, and retweet their news, they will start retweeting yours as well.

YouTube. Recruit a real estate agent to help you shoot video of your homes, communities, and happy homeowners. Try to post one video per month. You can also post videos on your blog or Facebook page. Those happy homeowners who just bought their second home from you would make a great video testimonial. Consider having an agent give a tour of one of the homes you recently completed; they could even interview the builder about favorite features of the home.

Campaign. Give to a nonprofit. Offer $1 for every new Facebook Like for a limited time or until you get a predetermined number of new fans. You can request that the potential beneficiary of your campaign promote it as well. Use all of your social media sites to promote the campaign but make sure they link to your Facebook page or blog. Several builders made charitable donations during the holidays using this strategy. Make sure to connect with the nonprofit before you start this type of campaign. If you find a social-media-savvy nonprofit, they will often help you promote the campaign through their sites and newsletters.

S&A Homes added a Salvation Army campaign to its Facebook page during the holidays. The builder donated one dollar for every new Like on the page. The company also added a Salvation Army app that allowed Facebook visitors to donate directly to the Salvation Army from the S&A Homes page.

Production Builders

Blog. Publish two or more stories a week (some builders post five days a week) as follows:

- **Promote your city.** Perhaps it recently made a top 10 list or is recognized for its quality of life.
- **Focus a series of posts around themes.**
  - First time home-buying tips that answer questions about issues such as mortgages, contracts, and taxes
  - Home organization from kitchens to garages and how your homes help organize buyers lives
  - Energy efficiency, including how your homes reduce energy bills, and tips for further savings.
- **Add videos** of all of your communities or individual home plans.
- **Discuss your credentials**, including Energy Star certification, and awards your company, homes, communities, or staff have won.

Facebook. Most production builders have set up one corporate Facebook page and a series of city specific pages for the markets where they build homes. Often these builders find the best results by having the corporate marketing department run the corporate page and selecting an online sales counselor or sales manager run their city-specific Facebook page. Post about your events, sales, area attractions, and new restaurants and shops near your communities.

Twitter. Tweet about incentives, sales, events, and area attractions. Connect with agents, mortgage bankers, and local retailers, and promote their events. They will promote yours in return. For example, you might tweet that the local cupcake store is offering two-for-one cupcakes today and that while they are in the area cupcake lovers should stop by your sales center: "2-4-1 cupcakes at @GigisCupcakes today, stop by Name of Community for water and a tour while u r there" (link to community's website). Chances are that the cupcake store will retweet your tweet.

For an incentive, try something like: "Going, Going, Gone. Today only free frig w/ purchase of Name of Home Model at Community" (link to community's website).

YouTube. Video possibilities are limited only by your imagination. Include model home tours, community walks, amenities in use, homeowner testimonials, and people enjoying your events. Interview coop agents who have sold more than one of your homes in a year about why they like working with you and what buyers like about your homes.

Campaigns. How about offering a free refrigerator or a similar option or upgrade to any buyer who checks into your community on Foursquare or a similar site? You also can offer percentage-off or dollars-off coupons to buyers who Like, follow, or check in to your community.

Custom Builder

Blog. Position yourself as the expert on luxury living in your city. Post photos of your amazing homes with your blog posts. Create content that ensures customers will choose you to build their custom home. You can discuss

- owner's suites;
- wine cellars;
- pools and spas;
- outdoor kitchens;
- home theaters;
- man caves;
- garages;
- exteriors; and
- windows and doors.

Support a local charity and ask your readers to participate with you. Sterling Custom Homes asked people to Like its Facebook page. For every new Like, the builder donated one dollar to the Make-A-Wish Foundation® of Central and South Texas. The builder gained 100 new fans and gave to a local charity. The Make-A-Wish Foundation promoted the program in its local newsletter.

Showcase homes under construction with photos and video. Consider shooting a walk-through video of the home at framing, drywall, and when the finishes start going in. These photos can pique the interest of potential buyers for the home or your next project. Make sure the images do justice for all of the details you include in the trim, fixtures, and finishes.

Facebook. Add the mobile Facebook application to your smartphone so you can post updates no matter where you are. Having the mobile app makes it so easy to respond to questions on your Facebook page from anywhere or change your status to reflect news. Add photos. Use your smartphone to snap a photo of a newly completed kitchen and upload it to your Facebook page with a post saying, "We just finished the kitchen at 1111 Gorgeous Home Drive in <u>Neighborhood</u>. Please call to tour the home." Or even a closing update, "We just closed another home. Congratulations to the new homeowners at 1111 Gorgeous Home Drive." Consider posting photos grouped by each area of the home to protect your homeowner's privacy. Your high-end homeowners don't want everyone that frequents your Facebook page to be able to tour their home room by room. Instead, create photo albums of many homes and group the photos by room or area, such as game rooms, pools, outdoor living, exterior elevations, gardens, living rooms, casitas, master suites, kitchens, and other areas. Reach out to real estate agents and your happy homeowners and ask them to Like your page. Strive to update your Facebook page once a week with a new blog post, a comment about a home under construction, more photos, or information on your current campaign.

Twitter. Add a mobile Twitter application to your smartphone so you can tweet while you wait for lunch, dinner, or in grocery store line. Here are some examples:

- Home at 1111 Gorgeous Home Drive sold today, congratulations to the new owners. (link to photo of home)
- It was nice to see <u>Agent Name</u> at our home today. Thanks for touring it with your customers.
- We just finished all the landscaping at 1111 Gorgeous Home Drive; now it's ready for move in. (link to home on website)

Include photos and links in your tweets and update your followers on projects and available home features. Twitpic (http://twitpic.com/) allows Twitter users to upload photos and video. You simply attach the photo to the tweet and Twitpic will incorporate it with a link to the image or video.

YouTube. Video is a great way for an out-of-town homeowner to follow the progress of a home under construction. Shoot footage and upload it to YouTube so your homeowners can review it. You can restrict viewers so only people you invite can see it. You can also shoot footage of homes under construction that are for sale and place those on your public YouTube channel.

Remodeler

Blog. Update your blog at least weekly and monitor it for comments. Following are some blog content ideas:

- Before and after photos of completed projects
- Tips for consumers considering a remodeling project
- Great products you've used in your projects and how they function
- Problems you have solved for homeowners with remodeling, such as making a bathroom accessible for aging in place
- Your designations, such as Certified Green Professional (CGP), Certified Aging in Place Specialist (CAPS), or Graduate Master Builder (GMB)

Facebook. Ask the people you want to follow you to connect. It's simple, but have you done it yet? To garner more referrals, incorporate a request for happy customers to Like you on Facebook into your closeout procedures for your remodeling projects.

If you've just started your Facebook page, send an *e-blast* to all of your clients asking them to follow your blog, Like you on Facebook, and follow you on Twitter. Exercise discretion with e-mail to avoid being labeled a spammer or breaking the law. Use an e-mail marketing program with an opt-out function like MailChimp (www.mailchimp.com), ConstantContact (www.constantcontact.com), or iContact (www.icontact.com) to help you comply with the CAN-SPAM Act. You should also

- Know the law
- Discuss the law with your attorney
- Monitor e-mail sent on your behalf

You are liable for your e-mail messages even if you have hired another company or person to send e-mail on your behalf.

Follow local real estate agents on Facebook and Twitter and ask them to follow you too. Many of the homes they sell will need remodeling.

Add photo albums for every project with before and after pictures and maintain photo albums by project type as well, such as bathrooms, kitchens, and additions.

Twitter. Create a Twitter account to tweet from your blog posts and to engage with real estate agents. To generate interest in following you, tweet valuable content, including tips on planning for a successful remodeling project. Link each tweet to your website or blog. Tweet about your remodeling passions, whether they are redesigning a kitchen, incorporating green features, creating luxurious master suites, or enabling homeowners to age in place.

YouTube. Videotape happy remodeling clients giving testimonials about your craftsmanship. You can load the videos on your blog and embed them in e-blasts.

Campaigns. Everyone wants a great deal. From Groupon to Facebook to foursquare, consumers are looking for coupons. What do you offer them to connect with you? Add a coupon to your blog or Facebook page for

- a free initial consultation;
- a free sink with a kitchen remodel; or
- 10% off an outdoor kitchen when you schedule by a certain date.

Social couponing sites are hot. Consumers want a good deal and they are willing to work to get it. Sites like Groupon offer daily deals of 50%–90% off on products and services.

Product Supplier

Blog. Publish new stories on your blog twice a week. Engage readers with lively prose, instead of just announcing a product release. For example, Construction Resources introduced its new frieze carpet as follows: "Frieze Carpeting: Shag Remixed? Can a remix ever be better than the original? It doesn't often happen that way in music, but when it comes to carpeting, frieze carpet has definite advantages over its older cousin, shag."

Here are some product topics worth blogging about:

- New product launches, new colors, new design elements or features
- Events, including open houses, online sales, and spring tent sales
- Eco-friendly, energy-saving, or other green product options
- Solutions for every price point
- On-time delivery and customer service, including testimonials
- Photos of completed installations

Facebook. Promote your events in advance and then follow up by posting photos. Remember to tag people who attend so the photo is on their page too. Post product news in an interesting way. For example, rather than writing a blatant sales pitch like "We have new frieze carpet in stock," use a rhetorical question and engage readers like this: "Remember shag carpet? Well, it's back in fashion, only now it's called frieze and it comes in much fresher colors. Please share your shag carpet memories with us."

Twitter. Follow your customers on Twitter and retweet their successes. Tweet about customer installations and cutting-edge aspects of your product, such as green features, aging-in-place functionality, low VOCs, recycled content, or time savings. Always link to your website, blog, or both, in your tweets.

YouTube. Showcase your product using video, from how it's made to how it's used to how it can solve specific problems. Include customer testimonials in your video library.

Campaigns. Why not offer a free sink if a customer buys 40 linear feet of countertop? Or a free spice pull-out with a new set of kitchen cabinets? Perhaps you could offer an upgrade on a faucet or toilet? Can you add an extra year of warranty? A free evaluation? A free spring HVAC check-up or other service? You are probably already offering specials like this, so add the buzz to your social sites.

Developing Content

Rich, relevant content is critical to attracting fans, followers, and visitors. Content demands planning. Your editorial calendar should include upcoming press releases, e-mail blasts, newsletter stories, and blog posts. When you create these items, repurpose them on online public relations sites and other blogs. Set your blog to populate your Facebook page and your Twitter account. These step-savers will ensure your social networking efforts are efficient.

Include news, award announcements, educational features, and community interest information in your press releases and blogs. Consumers are interested in tax credits, obtaining a mortgage, short sales, finding a custom builder, and remodeling their kitchen, among other topics.

Answer WIFM (What's in it for me?) in your content, tailoring subject matter for the particular audiences you want to reach. Your content must meet their needs or they won't follow you or engage you in conversation.

Social Media Policy

Now that your company is embracing social media, you need to create a *social media policy*. Your policy should provide an overview of why you are using social media and explain the goals of your social media strategy. A list of "don'ts" is not a comprehensive policy. Your policy should address employee behavior online, in general and specifically on social networking sites, especially as it relates to the company. Mashable recommends addressing the following 10 areas in a social media policy:[38]

1. Explain the purpose of social media.
2. Be responsible for what you write.

3. Be authentic.
4. Consider your audience.
5. Exercise good judgment.
6. Understand the concept of community.
7. Respect copyright and fair use.
8. Protect confidential proprietary information.
9. Add value.
10. Be productive.

Your company's social media policy should be unique, reflecting your culture and brand. Some companies are more liberal than others in who they allow to post and participate in their social media efforts. Neither a liberal nor a conservative approach is right or wrong.

As you make decisions, such as choosing the team to manage your social media marketing, remember the most important "rule" with SMM is consistency. Choose the team that can keep your program on track daily, weekly, and for the long haul.

Avoiding Pitfalls

Social media marketing has ramifications as well as rewards. The exponential nature of Internet communication can prove to be both a blessing and a curse. If you participate on third-party websites (sites you do not own), you are posting information that you cannot remove. Each blog post, tweet, and conversation will be seen by many, many users.

Self-Promotion

Shameless self-promotion never works well, but it is especially poorly received on social networking sites, where participants want to interact with their friends and favorite brands. Unlike *push advertising,* your posts should be conversational and provide interesting or valuable information to your community without overtly asking for a sale. Think of how you'd feel at a cocktail party if every time you turned around the same person handed you a business card and gave you a one-liner on his or her product or service. Social networking is no different! People are much more likely to friend, fan, or follow the person who provides useful information than the one who is always selling something.

One way to encourage interaction is to ask a question in your post. For example, rather than posting, "Facebook has changed the way it does feeds: There are now two options–top news and most recent," you might post "Facebook has changed its feeds to top news and most recent. I like the top news. Which do you like better?" Apply this same concept to posts about your communities, homes, remodeling projects, and news. For instance: "We've launched a new smaller series of ranch home plans, the Cypress, Vernon, and Hilary. Is single-level living attractive to you?"

Post With Discretion

Don't post or message too often. Often participants in social networks will accept your invitation to be your friend, fan, or follower for only a day or two. They try before they buy. But after a few days, they get tired of constantly finding your Facebook e-mails, incessant posts, and inappropriate tweets, so they walk away. Unfortunately, they are walking away from a relationship with your company.

On the other hand, some companies launch a disjointed social media presence without a strategy for maintaining their connections. Because social media then becomes too difficult or time-consuming to manage, they walk away from it. Abandoning your social media sites sends a negative message. Your contacts, friends, and followers may wonder if your business is struggling or defunct. Therefore, before you begin blogging, tweeting, and searching for networks, have a plan in place and a commitment to generating content that will build a positive brand.

Don't be afraid to cheer on your contacts. Like their posts on Facebook, and retweet good Twitter posts. Participate in the community by sharing but ensure you are up-to-date on the *netiquette* for each site so you don't respond inappropriately! For example, having an unfinished profile is a terrible offense on most sites. Don't start posting anywhere until you have built out your site. Posting without photos, descriptions, URLs, and contact information is like going to a networking event without business cards: you are unlikely to get follow-up.

Don't Be a Snark

The Urban Dictionary defines *snark* as a combination of "snide" and "remark," in other words a sarcastic comment, or a person who makes it. Don't be a snark even though becoming the target of a snark may be inevitable. (*Forbes* says the unhappy consumer group of *badvocates* represents about 20% of the world's adult population online and each one communicates his or her bad feelings to 14 people.[39])

Visiting http://www.RippOffReport.com, http://www.Yelp.com, http://www.city-data.com/forum/, or any number of other websites reveals the power of unhappy consumers. Because they are already conversing online even if you aren't there to hear it, you need to create places to embrace happy customers. Engage with both groups. Communication is the most important step toward building brand, creating transparency, and improving customer service.

Promoting Your Brand Online

Once you have built a team, written a plan, created a blog, improved your search results, and begun to use social networking sites, you are ready to netweave your online presence and promote it. Identify your objectives, the audiences you wish to reach, and where those people go online. Each home builder will adopt a unique strategy based on location, home types, home prices, and other factors.

Often, companies use free social networking sites to spread the word about other facets of their social media program. Just keep in mind that your goal is to use social media to build your business, not just to network because it's fun. Although social networking *is* fun, without goals it can also waste time and squander resources.

Every time you touch people online you make a brand impression. Impressions are also created when they visit your social sites. Whether it is a good impression or a bad impression depends on the quality of the interaction and how well you fulfill your company's brand promise. Take these seven steps to leave a good impression:

1. **Brand all of your sites with your colors, logo and information.** Make sure that visitors know they are visiting your official sites. For example, the Traton Homes logo is clearly displayed in the upper left hand corner of the Marietta, Georgia-based company's website and blog. Wherever it appears, the company logo uses consistent colors of red, blue, and tan.

2. **Develop messaging.** What is your brand promise? Whatever it is, make sure that everyone in the company understands the message and can successfully convey it to others on the spot face-to-face, on the phone, and in e-mail. Traton Homes stresses value by promising "Altogether More" (quality, location, lifestyle, and value) and longevity ("since 1971") in its brand promise.

   Kimberly Garwood, marketing manager of Traton Homes, says the "Altogether More" message affects everyone's job, from land development through design and construction, to sales and marketing. "Value is at the center of all of our process, messaging, and communication efforts," Garwood says.

3. **Post regularly on your social sites.** There is nothing worse than visiting a social site that has lain

dormant for months. Don't starve your social media program through neglect. This implies that you may be out of business. "A builder just launching a social media site should be aware that there is more to the process than just launching a site. It is an ongoing commitment that requires expertise and consistent development as it becomes a staple part of your marketing efforts," Garwood says. Chris Schoonmaker, vice president of sales for S&A adds, "Make it easy, but be committed to keeping it up to date. You have to post regularly to keep it fresh. The sites can't sit stagnant for months. Making sure to keep it fresh keeps the momentum going."

4. **Post unique content that will help define your brand.** Whether you build green, 50+, entry-level, luxury, or remodel within a particular niche, your unique selling proposition (USP) and your brand should be evident in your posts. "When you write more than 100 blogs about your company, you learn who you are, what your core competency is and what you do well. This gave us an excellent point to start from when we sat down to do the branding exercise. It made it easy because we absolutely know who we are," says Ashleigh Shetler, manager of sales and marketing development for S&A Homes in State College, Pennsylvania.

5. **Practice good customer service.** Make sure you respond to comments and questions on your social pages promptly, especially if they are negative, which they usually will not be. If you do get a negative post, simply respond, "I'm so sorry you are having a problem, This is <u>Name, Name of Company.</u> Please call me at <u>Direct-Dial Phone Number</u> so I can help you." This type of response will defuse the problem, keep it from escalating on your social site, and move it back to your traditional channels for handling customer complaints.

6. **Understand that your customers control your brand.** Your company will impress them either positively or negatively each time they interact with it. This extends far beyond your advertising, logo, and Internet marketing to include phone calls, e-mail, and the first introduction. Your customers need to know that they can trust your brand. "Social media has really forced builders to re-evaluate their entire marketing message—online, advertising, point of sale, product, everything. Because social media is so interactive, timely and up-to-date, it really forced S&A Homes to look at all of our advertising and take it to a more interactive level as well," Shetler says.

7. **Use a spokesperson, character, or icon to help define your brand.** It could be a supermodel or superhero, but it could also be a lovable pooch.

For example, Homer "works" for The Home Depot, Billy BadScore for Freescore.com, the Chick-fil-A cows for Chick-fil-A. You must admit that selling chicken sandwiches while focusing on cows is brilliant branding. Fully develop a persona and a voice for the spokesperson, whether a cartoon character or a live human being. Here are some examples of how your new spokesperson can become your number one brand advocate through social marketing.

Blogging. Give your spokesperson his or her own blog or a special category on your existing blog. This provides third-party credibility for the company by blogging about excellent customer service, special home features, community amenities, and home personalization.

Facebook. Update your corporate page to include your spokesperson in your company photo, perhaps standing in front of one of your homes or sitting inside the home he or she bought from you. If your spokesperson appears around town, mention the location in your status updates.

YouTube. Shoot videos of your spokesperson or incorporate them into videos with your sales agents, superintendents, and other staff. As your brand advocate, a spokesperson can interview happy homeowners, and interject positive comments as an owner of one of your homes.

Twitter. Have your brand spokesperson take over your Twitter account once a week, and share messages or host a Twitter chat.

"We probably approached this differently than many builders because instead of starting with a branding campaign, we [delved] into social media. We then realized how well it worked and that we needed to do this well with everything else we do. Now we are working to integrate social media through all of our advertising messages, including point of sale," Shetler says.

"We may not have as many followers, but the ones we have are really loyal. We have slowly and steadily built up our numbers of followers on the blog and Facebook," she says. "Now we are working to establish a two-way street between the blog and the website, so that both are strong online presences. It goes to show that it doesn't really matter where you are in the process, you can make social media work for you. When we first got started, we were really concerned that our website was not where it needed to be, but mRELEVANCE helped us build a strong social media program, and the state of the website didn't matter."

What are Shetler's tips for home builders getting ready to launch a social marketing program? "Make sure that whoever is responsible for implementing your social media program has a good handle on the company from finance to sales, marketing, events, who the company is, and what is going on in the company," she advises.

It can take years to build a brand and fulfill a brand promise. After all, the home buyers who live in homes will be experiencing your company's brand for years to come. Therefore, it is worth taking the time to do it right. Social marketing makes it easier than ever to either build or destroy your brand.

Maximizing E-mail and Newsletters

Use the following strategy to manage your e-mail and newsletter content and house it on the web:

- Post all of your content on your blog.
- Choose a few provocative sentences, or *teasers,* from each article to populate your newsletter template. Link to the complete story in the blog from these teasers.
- Use an e-mail service that allows you to send HTML newsletters and track clicks and opens. Tracking will show you who is most interested in your new community, new incentive, or other company news.
- Include links to all of your social media sites in your newsletter so that readers can Connect, Follow, and Like you on their chosen sites. Also, incorporate *social sharing* in your e-mail marketing so re-

cipients can forward e-mail content to their social networks. This will expand your newsletter's reach. Place social sharing links to popular social networks such as Twitter, Digg, Reddit, StumbleUpon, Facebook, Linkedin, and Yahoo! Buzz. A study by the e-mail marketing company GetReponse found that e-mail with social sharing options gets a 30% higher click-through rate than e-mails without options for sharing.[40] According to Marketing Sherpa,[41] 80% of marketers agree that social sharing extends e-mail content to new potential customers and increases brand awareness.

Sterling Custom Homes (fig. 7.1) creates its monthly newsletter using stories on its blog, http://www.Sterling CustomHomesBlog.com. Traffic to its website spikes for several days after the company distributes the newsletter.

Social Media on Your Website

Include social media icons with links on your website as well to make it easy for potential buyers to find information about your company. Consider displaying your company's telephone number on your home page. This communicates that you are out in front and ready to interact.

Figure 7.1 Sterling Custom Homes newsletter

Using blog stories as the basis for your newsletter saves times and streamlines the process while maximizing your ROI.

Source: Reprinted with permission from Sterling Custom Homes, Austin, Texas

Also place links to social media sites in your e-mail signatures. You don't have to include all of them you participate in, but rather just enough to point readers in the right direction. The four basic sites to includes are typically your blog, Facebook, Twitter and YouTube.

Your blog also should prominently display links to your social media sites as on Acadia Homes & Neighborhoods Homes blog (fig. 7.2), http://www.acadiahomes.us/news.com. This site is part of the company website structure. If your blog is a separate, stand-alone site, make sure that it provides a clear link to your main website. Also link all or most blog posts to a page on your website.

Make it easy for people to engage with your social networks. For example, the Greater Valley Group features Facebook prominently on its blog; visitors can Like the Facebook page without leaving the blog (fig. 7.3).

Even with the mass migration online, you still use print for some things. Include your social networking sites on yard signs, billboards, and business cards. When you comment on other companies' blogs and sites, include your website's URL to ensure that your post links back to your site.

Figure 7.2 Acadia Homes & Neighborhoods blog

Visitors to the Acadia Homes & Neighborhoods blog easily find links to all of the home builder social media sites.

Source: Reprinted with permission from Acadia Homes & Neighborhoods, Atlanta, Georgia.

Figure 7.3 Greater Valley Group Facebook page

One way to increase your company's following on Facebook is to add a Facebook Like box to your corporate website.

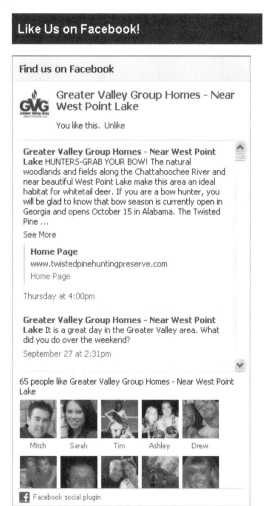

Source: Reprinted with permission from Greater Valley Group Properties, West Point, Georgia.

Social Media
and Customer
Relationship
Management

When potential buyers become friends, fans, or followers on social networking sites, they typically will observe more often than participate. By giving you access to a Twitter, Facebook, or other online profile, they're saying they're willing to listen and may want to talk, but they are not permitting you to add them to your database to send junk mail or spam.

So how should you respond to these friends, fans, or followers you want to convert to buyers? Meredith Oliver, MIRM, president of Raleigh, North Carolina-based Meredith Communications, an expert in lead follow-up and CRM for home builders, recommends

Sales and marketing functions are merging as a result of social media. Social media is the biggest innovation since the beginning of the Internet because it allows anyone to jump in and start a conversation. In this environment, sales is now marketing, and marketing is now sales. As a sales agent, you now have access to free online tools that you can use to build your business. Anyone in the company, from the president to the receptionist, can now build company brand online. Everyone can become an online sales counselor of sorts.

Now that anyone can set up interaction with potential home buyers, many sales agents must reinvent themselves and become advanced technology users. You must own and be adept using a smartphone; you must be agile at texting. To "click" with customers, you must be literate in the language they'll use to contact you.

With new opportunities come new urgencies, and agents can no longer take the time to get back to the office and follow up on a question or comment. In just four hours, an online inquiry becomes a cold lead. Smart phones, live chats, and speedy text messaging are the new must-haves in an agent's toolbox and skill repertoire.[42]

Buying Signals

In typical CRM systems, potential home buyers are categorized as leads, prospects, customers, or homeowners.

Your CRM system should recognize these different types of consumers by maintaining several mailing and do-not-contact lists. For example, just because you are interacting with a potential customer on Facebook does not mean that you can put them in your CRM program and start marketing to them through e-blasts. You could, however, add them to your CRM system just to note they are a Facebook connection. You could then keep track of your interactions with them there. Be careful not to turn off friends, fans, followers, or people who Like you by sending them marketing information before they opt-in to receive it. What does an opt-in look like when you are having a conversation on Facebook? It might be a subtle buying signal. Perhaps a person requested more information about the local school system or asked if there's a pool in the neighborhood. Someone might express interest in retail development or question the tax rate. These simple requests indicate the fan, friend, or follower is starting to imagine life in the community you are selling. This signals that you can add the person to your CRM system. Send a personal e-mail message sharing the benefits of receiving further correspondence from you and ask permission to send e-mail messages. If they decline, put them in a category of your CRM system for potential buyers who should be contacted only through the social networking medium in which they initiated the contact.

One the biggest benefits of a CRM system is the ability to provide everyone in your organization with a 360-degree view of a prospect. Everyone knows where prospects have visited (in person and online) and is privy to the information collected about them. Consider budget, company size, and functional requirements in choosing among the many CRM programs available. Among programs to evaluate are: Builder 1440, BuildTopia, Lasso, Pivotal, SalesForce, and Sales Simplicity.

Getting Social with CRM

The world is more social than ever. Social networks continue to transform how we do business and interact with customers, from one-way conversations to an interactive web of conversations. Finding out customer interests and ways to relate to them on a personal level is more important than ever.

To provide more detailed information on prospects and streamline communications, CRM systems are adding social media solutions to their programs. Look for new applications that allow users to integrate Facebook, Linkedin, Twitter, and other sites into CRM. For example, at least one CRM system enables users to post updates to their social accounts directly from the application. It allows users to find connections between prospects, customers, and decision-makers; find new opportunities through introductions; invite contacts and prospects to join social media sites; and track customer sentiment and engagement in the prospect database. The sales staff can see where the most recent contact with a prospect occurred, whether on Facebook, by e-mail, or through some other means, and what the prospect thinks of the company.

Follow-Up and Customer Service

Who will manage the company's responses to social media comments and questions depends entirely on the organization. Knowledge of social media is not the only prerequisite. People who interact with consumers online should have the following attributes:

- **Aptitude for customer service.** Your customer service representative, online sales counselor, or a technology-savvy agent already trained to work with the public would be good choices. The person must have a can-do attitude toward customers.
- **Skill and comfort with new technology.** Interacting through social websites requires not only familiarity with the sites as they exist now, but interest in new applications and devices such as smartphones and digital cameras.

- **Rapid response time.** People converse at the speed of life on social sites, and life moves quickly in today's technology-saturated world. In this context, a timely response means minutes, rather than hours. Failing to respond quickly could be the difference between a happy customer and a lost sale.
- **Solid grasp of the company's brand and USP.** To interact with customers, you want to make sure the person posting and answering their questions knows the answers to the questions that are most likely to be asked and can answer them in a way that keeps the customer personally engaged. There is nothing that consumers like less than being "sold" over a social network.

How to Measure Results

n the *Big Builder* survey discussed in chapter 1, respondents said their biggest concerns with social media were that it is too time consuming to manage (57.1%) and that there is no way to measure ROI (24.2%). But you can measure ROI if you know where to look for the information. Much of it will be in website tracking reports created at regular intervals by most Internet marketing firms.

Review your analytics and reports that track trends monthly and annually. An effective program will show slow, steady growth with some seasonal variation and sensitivity to economic conditions.

Ideally the messages your company distributes through social media outlets are reaching target audiences and will produce measurable results. How you measure your social media campaign's success depends on your goals. Following are suggestions for measuring ROI compared with the five goals for a social media marketing strategy discussed in chapter 2: increasing website traffic, social media optimization, reputation management, engagement, and building brand.

Goal 1: Increasing Website Traffic

After you implement the strategies discussed in this book, has the number of unique visitors to your site increased? Look behind and beyond the numbers. A plan to post significant content online with links referring to the company's main website probably was part of the strategy for reaching this goal. If the plan has been successful, your site visitors will come from a wider variety of searches and a larger number of referring URLs. You also may see more first-time site visitors than returning visitors.

Often, visitors who find your site through items you've posted or conversations you've started will be comparatively higher quality traffic: they visit more individual pages and spend more time on your site than other visitors. My own experience has shown that visitors who link to the mRELEVANCE LLC (http://www.mrelevance.com) site from our tweets tend to spend more time exploring the site than visitors from Facebook. Visitors from social media sites tend to spend three to six minutes on a site. Visitors from Twitter spend more time because they are coming with less information: they have based their visit on a 140-character tweet instead of a longer post on Facebook or on your blog.

Measurements for Goal 1: Increasing Website Traffic

1. Number of unique visitors
2. Time visitors spend on site
3. Number of pages visitors view
4. Number of referring URLs
5. Number of visitors who click through to "Contact Us" section
6. Increase in traffic from the search engines

Goal 2: Social Media Optimization

An SMO strategy focuses on increasing the number of relevant keywords that direct the search engines to your site and the number of referring sites that direct traffic to your site. Expand your keyword searches as follows:

Identify the terms site visitors already use to find the company.

Develop a list of USPs that visitors might use to find you through a search engine.

Post content focusing on these words in various places, and link to your site with anchor text. Your blog and any other online posts should include these keywords.

You should see an increase in the number of referring sites linking to your website. If the link is relevant and on highly visible sites, users are more likely to click it.

Measurements for Goal 2: Social Media Optimization

1. Number of keywords visitors use to find the site through search engines (fig. 9.1)
2. Quality of keywords (Do they reflect the company's USP and are they commonly searched?)
3. Number of referring sites (fig. 9.2)

Goal 3: Reputation Management

Businesses often undertake a reputation management program to push negative results from SERPs below the first screen or even deeper into search results. Posting positive, relevant content on online sites that rank highly in the search engines is an effective way to mitigate the negative publicity. How long it takes to improve first-page results depends on the power of the negative results.

Figure 9.1 Google Analytics results for Highland Homes

Google Analytics shows that 671 different keywords found Highland Homes during a 30-day period.

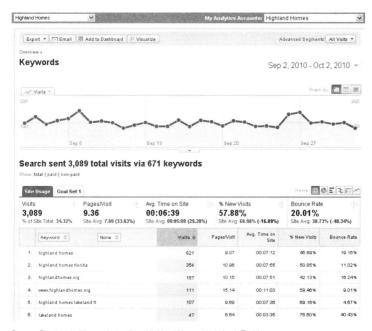

Source: Reprinted with permission from Highland Homes, Lakeland, Florida

Measurements for Goal 3: Reputation Management

1. Proportion of company-generated information in page one search results

Figure 9.2 Highland Homes referring sites

Google Analytics shows that during a 30-day period, referring sites sent 1,986 visits from 224 sources to the Highland Homes website.

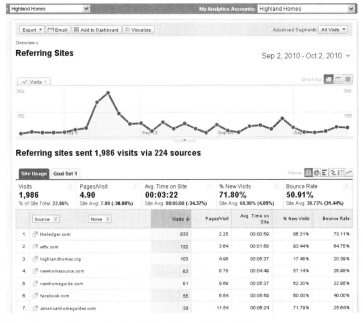

Source: Reprinted with permission from Highland Homes, Lakeland, Florida

2. Negative search engine results moved to page two or lower of SERP

Goal 4: Social Networking

The goal of social networking is to engage target audiences in conversation. Specific target audiences will vary by company and may even vary by the social networking tool used. Most of these tools keep tabs on the people subscribing to the user's content, whether they call them friends, followers, or fans. The quality of your followers is much more important than the quantity. Therefore, if you aren't following people who can buy from you or influence the buying decision of a potential customer, rethink your strategy.

To monitor the conversation, you can hire a social media monitoring company from among those listed at http://tinyurl.com/6zeq9u9 or you can create free alerts through Google Alerts to see what others are saying.

Measurements for Goal 4: Social Networking

1. Number of friends/followers/fans
2. Number of friends/followers/fans in your target audiences (for example homeowners, real estate agents, home buyers, influencers)

3. Quality of conversations (Are friends/followers/fans just receiving content, or are they actually engaged and participating?)

Goal 5: Building Brand

Strategies for building brand are similar to those for SMO. You want to ensure that potential customers can find you online and that what they find represents your company honestly. If your company name is not unique, you must ensure that your brand appears high in the SERP results with a message that differentiates you from other companies with the same name.

Measurements for Goal 5: Building Brand

1. Combined measures for SMO and reputation management.
2. Increased USPs represented in keywords. If you are a green builder in Denver, for example, when local consumers search for green homes in Denver your company should rank high on the SERP.
3. Positive representations of the company in many places online.

Ultimate Goal: Sales

If your social media program is successful in meeting goals 1–5, then you probably will achieve your ultimate goal: sales. With most home buyers researching markets and builders online, the entire social media network is influencing home sales. Following are three examples– of a builder and two developers–that translated social media into increased website traffic, more leads, and ultimately, more sales.

Highland Homes

Highland Homes of Lakeland, Fla., transformed a primarily print-based advertising campaign to an Internet-focused marketing campaign in 2008. Like all home builders faced with fewer sales, slower traffic, and reduced margins, Highland Homes had to find ways to achieve sales with a smaller budget. By 2010, Highland Homes had cut its marketing budget by 80% from its high, but was still selling homes using a strategic Internet-focused marketing program. The builder even expanded into new markets in 2010.

One interesting outcome is that Internet conversion has increased over the life of the program from 13 to 33%. Overall, Highland Homes averaged 43 contracts a month in 2010.

Highland Homes first hired mRELEVANCE in January 2008 to keep its website alive. The mRELEVANCE team rewrote the entire site in a different programming language, optimized the site for the search engines, and was in the midst of changing and updating the content when the home builder made a first round of budget cuts.

Kathie McDaniel, broker, MCSP, MIRM, vice president of sales and marketing for Highland Homes, says, "The business intelligence provided by the monthly analytics reports from mRELEVANCE helps our team strategize on where to focus marketing dollars and time." She continues, "As we focus on areas that are most effective, we have been able to increase our traffic to both our website and models while at the same time increasing the Highland Homes brand. When our budget decreased, our biggest cutbacks were in print advertising–going from full-page, four-color weekly placements to quarter or half page."

At the same time, Highland Homes maintained a strong online presence with listing ads and banners in many places. One of the builder's top sources of traffic to its website is online banner ads on Yahoo.

Strategy

mRELEVANCE launched an SMM campaign to maintain brand, build online reputation, and enhance Highland Homes' search engine marketing. The campaign sought to use SMO to increase keywords and referring URLs for the Highland Homes website by

- building a blog;
- using external blogs;
- creating a Facebook page; and
- using other social networking, online public relations, and social bookmarking sites.

The blog launched as the news section of the builder's main website. It contains community news, events, and information on sales and the builder's team. Social networking sites, such as Facebook, Twitter, and ActiveRain, increased exposure within those communities. Online public relations sites filled the SERP results with positive news. Social Bookmarking and e-mail marketing supported the entire campaign.

Here are the results:

- 80% increase in keywords by 2010 compared with a 20% increase the first year
- 60% increase in referring URLs by 2010 compared with a 25% increase the first year
- 110% increase in overall web traffic by 2010 compared with 26% the first year
- 60% increase in Internet leads by 2010 compared with 53% the first year
- 33% conversion rate of Internet leads to home purchase contracts in 2010 compared with 13% in 2009

Highland Homes has embraced social media as a critical piece of its marketing strategy. "Since our marketing budget was cut we have definitely had to work smarter. Our social media campaign has given us a way to increase our search engine optimization and traffic to our website, and interact with our buyers. mRELEVANCE keeps the strategy moving forward with blogs and posts, while the Highland Homes team tweets and posts the day-to-day news and sales stats," McDaniel says.

The most significant change in the social media program from 2009 to 2010 was an increased presence on YouTube, including a tour of the company's Personal Selection Studio. The virtual tour has drawn new prospects to Highland Homes and helped faraway clients make selections remotely. "It has really helped us build sales," McDaniel says.

Greater Valley Group

Greater Valley Group launched an interactive campaign in 2010 as a method for the West Point, Georgia, developer to increase traffic to its websites, improve SEO, and reach a broader audience through the Internet while reducing overall marketing expenditures.

Greater Valley Group is a residential and commercial developer with a number of projects, including hotels, apartment complexes, condominiums, single family homes, retail and other commercial office buildings, industrial properties, and lot and land opportunities. The Greater Valley area which includes Lanett and Valley, Ala., as well as West Point, is experiencing rapid growth with the recent opening of the new Kia Motors Manufacturing Georgia plant in West Point.

mRELEVANCE built a program for the developer including a number of blog websites, including

- http://www.GVGRealEstate.com, the main news blog (fig. 9.3);
- http://www.GVGHome.com, a site for residential sales; and
- http://www.GVGHold.com, a site for residential, retail, and commercial development.

With its wide variety of products and price points, Internet shoppers had to be able to find the developer through multiple sites. The online program also extended the lifespan of the budget for the projects while reaching a number of key audiences—those relocating to work for Kia, active military, and retirees.

A website tracking report follows the developer's Internet program. The Internet-focused strategy includes search engine optimization, a social media marketing program, online public relations, online banner

Figure 9.3 Greater Valley Group blog

The Greater Valley Group blog promotes event news of interest to those living in the area, as well as those looking to visit West Point lake.

Source: Reprinted with permission from Greater Valley Group Properties, West Point, Georgia.

advertising, pay-per-click, e-mail marketing, and landing pages and contact forms on various websites.

Strategy

mRELEVANCE used many strategies in the Greater Valley Group SMM campaign, including the following:

A custom Greater Valley Group real estate blog (http://www.GVGRealEstate.com). The blog shares news on communities and area activities, and tips for home buyers on tax credits, home loans, and related topics. The blog includes comprehensive information on the Greater Valley area, including stories about the opening of a new restaurant, Shuckers on the Cove, and events like Adventure Jam, an outdoor competition which includes 12 miles of mountain biking, 5 miles of trekking, and 2 miles of team canoeing or individual kayaking. Sixty to seventy-five percent of the blog's traffic is new visitors. Diverse content attracts a wide variety of Internet searches through hundreds of keywords. The blog is among the top referral sources for the GVGHome website (http://www.GVGHome.com), the developer's residential real estate site. Visitors from that site spend an average of more than four minutes on the site and view more than five pages.

"We felt it was very important to launch a blog that included detailed and up-to-date information not only about Greater Valley Group, but also the Greater Valley Area," said Tim Randolph, COO of Southern Place Homes, an affiliate of the Greater Valley Group. "In today's technology-driven world, it is imperative to have an online presence to ensure visitors who are looking for reliable information about us and our community can find it easily."

External blogs such as Atlanta Real Estate Forum, ActiveRain, Luxury Real Estate, Fifty Plus Housing, and GeorgiaGolf Living, comprise a major component of the SMO program for Greater Valley Group. One of GVGHome's best referral sources is http://www.AtlantaRealEstateForum.com. The site refers visitors who view multiple pages and spend roughly 2 minutes on GVGHome.

Both the GVGHome and GVGHold (http://www.GVGHold.com) websites were rebuilt as blog websites, which greatly increased the amount of traffic to both sites as well as the number of keywords associated with them. The main blog, http://www.GVGRealEstate.com, attracts out-of-state traffic. In September 2010 the blog had visitors from 27 states.

The campaign also incorporates online PR, social networking, and other strategies discussed previously. Here are the results:

- Page 1 SERP results for a number of keywords, such as "homes near Kia" and "West Point Lake real estate" are excellent.
- Keyword phrases increased by 65% for GVGHome.
- Referring traffic increased by 25% for GVGHome.
- Keyword phrases increase by 66% for GVGHold.
- Referring traffic increased by 25% for GVG Hold.

B.F. Saul

B.F. Saul, the developer of Circle 75 Townhomes in Smyrna, Georgia, turned to search engine optimization, social media, discounting, and a targeted Realtor e-flyer campaign in mid-2009 to propel the sale of its final 48 units.

The Circle 75 news blog (fig. 9.4) launched in July 2009 as the foundation of the social media and online marketing program. Through the use of targeted keywords and search engine optimization, the blog attracted more than 2,600 unique visitors, creating a bigger lead funnel for converting Internet browsers to home buyers.

Traffic to the main Circle 75 website increased by more than 600% from January 2009 to January 2010 and more than 500% from February 2009 to February 2010. Overall, website traffic during the campaign—from June 2009 to February 2010—increased by more than 400%.

The target market was first-time townhome buyers in Cobb County. Marketing objectives were straightforward: increase keywords, website traffic, and sales. The community sold out within eight months of launching the blog.

The blog improved the community's search engine optimization by capturing more keywords for the main website (a 175% increase). Overall website traffic

Figure 9.4 Circle 75 blog

The Circle 75 Blog attracted a wide range of searches on a variety of keywords.

Source: Reprinted with permission from B.F. Saul Company, Bethesda, Maryland

increased by more than 450%. The blog enhanced the community's Internet presence. Blog posts talked up the community and area events, and highlighted community attractions such as Smyrna Market Village and the community's hip Smyrna–Vinings location.

S&A Homes

S&A Homes actively builds homes in 65 communities throughout Pennsylvania and West Virginia. With a number of different product types and styles suitable for many demographics, S&A had to find a way to stretch its marketing dollars. The company hired mRelevance to launch a social media marketing program. The campaign used online resources to showcase S&A homes, communities, and locations to increase the probability that today's technology-savvy home buyers and real estate agents would find S&A homes online, get to know the builder, and ultimately, buy an S&A home.

S&A Homes launched its social media campaign in July 2010 with three main goals:

1. Increase website traffic.
2. Create a place for consumers to converse with the builder.
3. Improve the SEO for its main website.

"We saw excellent early results. Within 45 days of launch the blog was already a top five referral source to our main website with 75% of the traffic on the blog representing first time visitors." said Ashleigh Shetler, manager of sales and marketing development for S&A Homes. "The blog continues to perform well. The blog was the number two referral site to our website with first-time visitors from the blog to the website representing 50% of the traffic [in a 30-day period]."

Google and Facebook are the top referring sites to the blog. Several other blogs and social media sites also send traffic to the blog, including Twitter. Keywords on the blog have grown from several dozen a month to more than 350 a month. Best of all, the blog metrics of visitors, keywords, referring sites, and overall traffic continue to grow each month.

S&A Homes Tool Kit

S&A Homes focused on four main social media tools:

1. **Blog** (http://www.sahomesblog.com/). The S&A Homes blog is built on a self-hosted WordPress platform. The blog's editorial calendar is planned several months out, and content focuses on topics from energy-efficient homes to tips for first-time buyers, home organization ideas, community events, and community news. The blogging team consists of members from both the S&A Homes team and mRELEVANCE. The blog's goal is to provide enticing content that also maximizes SEO. Blog categories include news, events, incentives, videos, testimonials, and locations. Each of these also has categories for S&A Homes' various community locations. The blog's home page features a

video that allows visitors instant access to views of S&A homes.

2. **Facebook** (http://www.facebook.com/sahomes). We all want to go where everybody knows our name, and Facebook is definitely the neighborhood watering hole where everyone shares news and information. S&A Homes utilizes its Facebook page to connect with and engage homeowners, home buyers, and real estate agents. Facebook content must be fresh, so S&A updates the page automatically with blog news as well as posts unique to the Facebook page. The S&A Homes Facebook page invites first-time home buyers with a link to a comprehensive section on the company's blog that answers many questions that first-time buyers have. Hundreds of people Like the page and many of them actively participate by commenting, which makes the page feel like a community, rather than just a commercial website.

3. **YouTube** (http://www.youtube.com/SAhomebuilder). If a picture is worth a thousand words, a video must be worth a million. The S&A Homes YouTube page showcases communities and home plans. Many of these videos are embedded into blog posts as well. Sales agents can follow up with prospects by e-mailing them links to the videos.

4. **Twitter** (http://twitter.com/SAhomebuilder). S&A uses Twitter to further syndicate blog posts and promote campaigns, although the main focus of Twitter is to interact with agents and industry influencers. Future Twitter plans include promoting a Lab Home and E-home, as well as sharing first-time buying information.

Campaigns

Understanding that great content is not always enough to encourage online interaction, much less an action, S&A Homes initiated several targeted social media campaigns to encourage online participation. The company has chosen to build a smaller, core group of followers who are genuinely interested in S&A Homes, instead of a larger group of followers that is simply chasing companies for contest monies. Its campaigns reflect that philosophy.

$1,500 off Options and Upgrades. The first campaign, a 45-day, $1,500 off options and upgrades promotion, launched on July 15, 2010. Blog posts and Facebook posts encouraged potential buyers to Like the S&A Homes Facebook page and to download a coupon for $1,500 off S&A Homes Options with the purchase of a new home (fig. 9.5). Buyers could use the coupon in conjunction with other incentives. E-mail messages also promoted the campaign. When the promotion was over, customers had redeemed

Figure 9.5 **S&A Homes $1,500 upgrade incentive**

S&A Homes promoted its Facebook coupon through a blog post.

Source: Reprinted with permission from S&A Homes, State College, Pennsylvania

six coupons. You can visit the blog post for the promotion at http://www.sahomesblog.com/2010/07/sa-homes-to-deliver-savings-to-facebook-fans/.

Operation Organize Simplify. Building on the success of the coupon campaign, S&A Homes launched "Operation Organize Simplify" in mid October 2010. This campaign targeted potential home buyers and Realtors® with a multifaceted program including blog posts (fig 9.6), Facebook and e-mail blasts. "Operation Organize Simplify" focused on the benefits of home design to simplify your life. Blog posts discussed kitchen storage, laundry rooms, charging stations, drop zones, and even the ultimate man room–the garage.

To engage real estate agents and tap into their expertise, the blog asked them, "If you could build your dream home, what is the one organizational item that you would incorporate into every home?" Agents competed for a $150 gift card to Home Depot and the opportunity to receive a $500 bonus at their next S&A Homes closing. Agents submitted creative organization strategies for Christmas tree rooms, kitchen electronics, and the ultimate mudroom.

Meanwhile, home buyers could download a coupon that could be redeemed for $1,500 off of organizational options on their presale new home purchase. Buyers redeemed six coupons during the 45-day campaign.

"After these home buyers signed contracts for their new homes, they took time to Like us on Facebook,"

Figure 9.6 S&A Homes Operation Organize Simplify

S&A Homes promoted its Operation Organize Simplify campaign through the blog.

Source: Reprinted with permission from S&A Homes, State College, Pennsylvania

said Ashleigh Shetler, manager of sales and marketing development. This is big in terms of future referrals from these buyers via Facebook.

You can view the Operation Organize Simplify blog post at http://www.sahomesblog.com/2010/10/how-do-you-organize-your-life/.

Life is Full of Firsts. To demonstrate that buying a first home should be as special as a first kiss, first date, or your child's first day of school, S&A Homes launched a promotion, "Life is Full of Firsts," geared toward educating first time buyers (fig. 9.7). Blog content aims to demystify home buying for the first-timer by providing a "buying 101" primer. It addresses topics such as FHA loans, mortgage interest deductions, USDA financing, the benefits of new construction instead of a used home, tax benefits of owning, and how to own with no money down. The Life is Full of Firsts promotion for first-time buyers is also set up as the Facebook landing page to encourage potential buyers to get the information they need and make educated home purchasing decisions.

Scorecard

Eight months after starting the social media program, S&A Homes reports the program performed better than the home builder expected. "Our social media

Figure 9.7 **S&A Homes Life is Full of Firsts campaign**

S&A Homes educated first time buyers through a campaign designed specifically for them.

Source: Reprinted with permission from S&A Homes, State College, Pennsylvania

program has exceeded our expectations. It has brought new visitors to our website, improved the SEO for our main website, created a place where consumers can have conversations and best of all, it has brought us buyers!" says Shetler. "We had 12 homebuyers redeem coupons for options and upgrades that they could have gotten only on our social media sites. There is no doubt that today's buyers are looking further than just our website. We will continue to provide them with ways to interact with us and reward them for their loyalty."

Used effectively, social media marketing is a tremendously powerful marketing tool. Companies can raise their online visibility, improve SEO, increase the number of qualified leads, connect with customers and prospects, and ultimately, sell more homes, jobs, and products. Embracing this medium to reach out to potential buyers is a necessary step toward successfully marketing and selling your homes today.

Planning a Strategy

N ow you know that SMM is much more than just having a Facebook page! You must provide customers with real-time interactive assistance across multiple devices—from smartphones to tablets to PCs. In other words, companies need to be where their customers are and ready to meet their needs immediately. I've shown you how using SMM can dramatically increase your visibility and help you sell more homes. You can create a strategy to use this powerful and popular medium to reach buyers.

First, assemble a team because one person in your marketing department can't do it alone. Train everyone in your company to participate in your social media program so they are empowered to successfully use websites to reach target audiences. Get your sales team to participate in your social marketing. Because they interact daily with your customers they need access to all the social media accounts and training to use the accounts effectively. And with the sales and marketing functions becoming more closely aligned than ever, real estate agents have a tremendous stake in the success of the home builders they represent.

After your team is in place, make sure your website is interactive. Once you get your successful social media program off the ground, there is nothing worse than directing interested customers to a boring, static website. Make sure yours is engaging enough that they will stay long enough to find the information they need and perhaps even contact you for more information. Then take the following steps:

- Establish goals for your SMM strategy and write them down.
- Purchase necessary tools, such as a smartphone and digital camera.
- Launch a blog.
- Create an editorial calendar.
- Repurpose press releases, e-flyers, and other marketing materials for various online channels.
- Contribute to real estate/industry blogs.
- Create pages on social networking sites.
- Interact in the social media sphere and build lists of agents, prospects, customers, and influencers.
- Send strategic e-blasts. Establish a schedule for distributing e-mail messages on a consistent basis. This could vary from quarterly to weekly depending on the size of your company and the number of audiences to whom you send e-mail. Use software that allows recipients to opt-out and has

analytics for you to measure your success and de-termine how to follow up.

- Track results and update your strategy as needed. Tracking what works and what doesn't allows you to make smarter marketing decisions. You will be able to analyze results and make changes monthly and perhaps even weekly.

Figures 10.1 and 10.2 are sample plans and work-sheets for the first and second months of your strategy.

Month One

The size of your program and of your implementation team may warrant spending two months, rather than just one, on this setup phase. In this phase, you will cre-ate your strategy, establish your social media policy, and begin to build your social media presence as follows:

- Create your strategy.
- Set realistic, measurable goals.
- Determine keywords.
- Create an editorial calendar.
- Build your online presence.
  - ○ Blog
  - ○ Social networks
  - ○ Online PR sites

Figure 10.1 Sample plan for month one

Focus on setting up all accounts and interconnecting them during the first month.

Company Name			
Project	**Status**	**Assigned**	**Link (if applicable)**
Month, Year			
Strategy	complete		
Goals	complete		
Determine keywords	complete		
Create editorial calendar	In process		
Build blog			
Create Facebook page			
Create Twitter account			
Create ActiveRain account			
Create Trulia account			
Update YouTube channel			
Review/Update Linkedin page			
Create Flickr account			
Create PR.com			
Create Networked Blog account			
Import blog into Facebook page			
Connect blog to Twitter			
Research external sites and blogs			
Netweave—add buttons and links			
Set up website & blog tracking			
Set up Google Alerts™			
Set up other tracking— Twitter, etc.			
Review Google Analytics™ and create baseline			

Figure 10.2 **Sample plan for month two**

Developing and posting content is the focus of month two.

Date, Year	Status	Assigned	Link
Complete Tracking Report for previous month			
News Release #1			
Post on PR.com			
Post on PressReleasePoint			
Post on PRLog			
Post on NHDBuzz			
Repurpose for NewHomesSection			
Post on Yahoo Buzz			
Repurpose for Activerain			
Repurpose for Trulia			
Repurpose to Local Niche blog			
Repurpose for Local Industry blog			
News Release #2			
Post on PR.com			
Post on PRWeb			
Post on PRFree			
Post on NHDBuzz			
Bookmark on Delicious			
Repurpose for Activerain			
Repurpose on Trulia			
Repurpose to Local Niche blog			
Repurpose for Local Industry blog			
Blog Posts			
1 - Repurpose News Release #1	Wk 1		
2 - Community Info	Wk 1		
3 - Homebuying Info	Wk 2		
4 - Community Info	Wk 2		
5 - Repurpose News Release #2	Wk 3		
6 - Homebuying Info	Wk 3		
7 - Community Info	Wk 4		
8 - Community Info	Wk 4		
Other Sites			
Linkedin – update personal status to link to a blog post with a shortened URL			
Linkedin – make comments on others announcements, make referrals, seek new connections, make sure employees are listed on corporate profile			
Twitter – develop a schedule of what to tweet in between the 8 tweets from the blog			
Twitter – add relevant followers			
Facebook – develop a schedule of posts for in between the 8 posts from the blog			
Facebook – interact with agents, add relevant Friends and convert them to Fans			
Update Flickr pages - add new photos			
Update Facebook - add new photos			
Train agents on how to tweet, RT, etc.			
Answer Q&As on Trulia			
Join groups on Active Rain			
Comment on other industry blogs			

- Research external blogs and sites. Find one or two sites to contribute to and enlist guest experts to blog on your site.
- Netweave all sites with buttons, logos, feeds, and applications.
- Track results.
- Set up analytics for the website and blog and create baseline reports.
- Set up Google Alerts.
- Create Twitter searches.
- Consider purchasing a social media monitoring program.

Month Two

As you move into month two and beyond, you'll settle into a routine of pushing your marketing messages out, monitoring the response, and interacting with your online community. Listen, engage, and respond appropriately!

- Disseminate two press releases.
- Post online to PR sites.
- Repurpose and post on other external sites.
- Post eight blog entries.
    - Create two by repurposing press releases.
    - Discuss overall housing news in two.
    - Focus on community news or company news in the other four.

- Link to the press releases and blog posts from your Facebook page and Twitter account.
- Post at least four messages on external blogs.
- Comment on two blogs.
- Seek new Facebook fans and Twitter connections weekly.
- Post on Facebook.
- Interact on Twitter.
- Add photos and video to Flickr and YouTube.
- Train sales associates and outside agents on using Facebook, Linkedin, blogs, and other social media and social networking sites.
- Monitor websites and respond to questions and comments.
- Review progress toward goals and adjust strategy and tactics as necessary.

Larger companies may need to add to these sample plans, whereas smaller builders may wish to scale them back. Once you determine the strategy and staffing that works best for your company, SMM will become part of your marketing routine just as updating pricing or planning for weekend signage is.

SMM will continue to change and evolve. However, your blog will remain the hub of your program. With your own self-hosted WordPress blog, you won't have to rely on the ever-changing social networks to get your message out. Your blog is the component of your program that you own and control. A well-built blog will be one of your website's top referring sites.

As you build your program, please friend, fan or follow me and let me know how it is going. I'm easy to find: just Google my name or look for me at http://www. mRELEVANCE.com, http://www.CarolFlammer.com, http://Twitter.com/AtlantaPR or http://www.Facebook. com/CarolFlammer. I'm on lots of other sites too. If you don't find me where you are, shoot me an old fashioned e-mail and ask me to join you!

Notes

1 Harris Interactive, "2005 New Home Buyer and Home Builder Survey Executive Summary," 2006, http://newhomesresource.move.com/News/Include/IRM%20Research%20Executive%20Summary%20PDF%203-8-06.pdf.

2 Paul Chaney. The Digital Handshake: Seven Proven Strategies to Grow Your Business using Social Media. Hoboken, NJ: John Wiley & Sons, Inc., 2009.

3 "MarketingSherpa and TechWeb Business Technology Buyer Survey," (Warren, RI: MarketingSherpa LLC, September 2009), http://www.marketingsherpa.com/.

4 Sarah Yaussi, editor, Big Builder, in personal communication with the author, April 2009.

5 Audience poll, NAHB Professional Women in Building webinar, June 10, 2010, http://www.nahb.org/generic.aspx?sectionID=1103&genericContentID=139679&print=true.

6 eMarketer, "Steady Gains in Blogging by Marketers," August 17, 2010, http://www.emarketer.com/Article.aspx?R=1007871.

7 Mary Madden, "Older Adults and Social Media," Pew Research Center Publications, August 27, 2010, http://pewresearch.org/pubs/1711/older-adults-social-networking-facebook-twitter.

8 Linda Boland Abraham, Pauline Morn Marie, and Andrea Vollman, "Women on the Web: How Women are Shaping the Internet," comScore, June 2010, http://www.comscore.com/layout/set/popup/request/Presentations/2010/Women_on_the_Web_PDF_Request?

req=slides&pre=Women+on+the+Web%3A+How+Women+are+ Shaping+the+Internet.

9   Susan Wright and Elisa Camahort Page, "2009 Women and Social Media Study," BlogHer, iVillage, and Compass Partners, April 2009, http://www.npd.com/lps/Entertainment_Trends2009/.

10 Richard H. Levey, "Survey Shows Gender Differences In Retail Social Media Use," www.ChiefMarketer.com, January 4, 2011, http://chiefmarketer.com/social/metrics/gender-difference-retail-social-media-011211/?cid=nl_cm_direct.

11 Dan Schawbel, "The Top 10 Social Networks for Generation Y," www.Mashable.com, January, 30, 2009, http://mashable.com/ 2009/01/30/generation-y-social-networks/.

12 Ian Shapira, "In a Generation That Friends and Tweets, They Don't," *Washington Post,* October, 15, 2009, http://www.washingtonpost.com/ wp-dyn/content/article/2009/10/14/AR2009101403961.html.

13 Facebook Statistics, http://www.facebook.com/press/info.php? statistics, accessed October 2, 2010.

14 Peter Corbett, "Facebook Demographics and Statistics Report 2010–145% Growth in 1 Year," January 4, 2010, http://www.istrategy labs.com/2010/01/facebook-demographics-and-statistics-report-2010-145-growth-in-1-year/.

15 YouTube Fact Sheet, http://www.youtube.com/t/fact_sheet, accessed October 2, 2010.

16 The Huffington Post, "Twitter User Statistics REVEALED," April 30, 2010, http://www.huffingtonpost.com/2010/04/14/twitter-user-statistics-r_n_537992.html.

17 Technorati State of the Blogosphere 2010, http://technorati.com/ blogging/article/state-of-the-blogosphere-2010-introduction/, accessed March 5, 2011.

[18] Perez, Sarah. "Smartphones Outsell PCs," February 8, 2011, http://www.readwriteweb.com/archives/smartphones_outsell_pcs.php.

[19] Gahran, Amy. "Report: 90% of Americans own a computerized gadget," February 3, 2011, http://www.pewinternet.org/Media-Mentions/2011/Generations-and-gadgets-CNN.aspx.

[20] Levinson, Mitch. Managing Partner, mRELEVANCE, in personal communication with the author, October 2009 and October 2010.

[21] WordPRess.org, "Free Themes Directory," http://wordpress.org/extend/themes/browse/popular/, accessed March 19, 2011.

[22] The Official Google Blog, "Our new search index: Caffeine," June 8, 2010, http://googleblog.blogspot.com/2010/06/our-new-search-index-caffeine.html.

[23] S&A Homes Blog, "S&A Homes Offers E-Incentive for Realtors," August 23, 2010, http://www.sahomesblog.com/2010/08/sa-homes-offers-e-incentive-for-realtors/.

[24] Chicagoland Real Estate Forum, "4 Tips to Improve Your Credit Score," September 13, 2010, http://www.chicagolandrealestateforum.com/2010/09/13/4-tips-to-improve-your-credit-score/.

[25] Parks, Chris. "The $6^{1}/_{2}$ Best Reasons Not to Build a Boone Home," March 19, 2010, http://www.boonehomesblog.com/builder-news/custom-home-builder-boone-homes/.

[26] Spencer, Laura, "Laundry—the Easy Way," June 16, 2010, http://www.boonehomesblog.com/builder-news/laundry-the-easy-way/.

[27] Quenqua, Douglas, "Blogs Falling in an Empty Forest" *The New York Times,* June 5, 2009, http://www.nytimes.com/2009/06/07/fashion/07blogs.html?_r=2.

[28] U.S. Copyright Office, "Fair Use," accessed January 28, 2011, http://www.copyright.gov/fls/fl102.html.

[29] Google Webmaster Central, "Duplicate content," http://www.google.com/support/web1ST REVISE/bin/answer.py?hl=en&answer=66359, accessed October 2, 2010.

[30] Brunswick, "Social Media Survey," http://www.brunswickgroup.com/insights-analysis/surveys.aspx, March 11, 2011.

[31] Abramovich, Giselle, "Vast majority of journalists look for news online," www.DMNews.com, (New York: Haymarket Media Inc., July 26, 2007), http://www.dmnews.com/vast-majority-of-journalists-look-for-news-online/article/97998/.

[32] The George Washington University, "National Survey Finds Majority of Journalists Now Depend on Social Media for Story Research," January, 21, 2010, http://www.gwu.edu/explore/mediaroom/news releases/nationalsurveyfindsmajorityofjournalistsnowdependon socialmediaforstoryresearch.

[33] Kunar Patel, "How Your Likes Are Turning Facebook Into the Loyalty Card of the Internet," Advertising Age, September 20, 2010, http://adage.com/digital/article?article_id=145982.

[34] Shannon Manso, Sales Manager, BHI, in personal communication with the author, October 2009.

[35] comScore, "The 2010 Mobile Year in Review," http://www.com score.com/layout/set/popup/request/Presentations/2011/2010_ Mobile_Year_in_Review_PDF_Request?req=slides&pre=The+2010 +Mobile+Year+in+Review, February 2011.

[36] eMarketer, "Mobile Users Ready for Location-Based Text Marketing," http://www.emarketer.tv/Article.aspx?R=1007782&Aspx AutoDetectCookieSupport=1, July 26, 2010.

[37] Loechner, Jack. "Almost as Good as a Sandwich Board," *Media Post: Online Media Daily,* October 27, 2009. http://www.mediapost.com/publications/?fa=Articles.showArticle&art_aid=116066.

[38] Sharlyn Lauby, "10 Must-Haves for Your Social Media Policy," Mashable: The Social Media Guide, June 2, 2009, http://mashable.com/2009/06/02/social-media-policy-musts/.

[39] Laurie Burkitt, "Marketers Grapple with Brand-Bashing 'Bad-vocates'," (New York: Forbes.com LLC®, October 23, 2009), http://www.forbes.com/2009/10/23/general-motors-american-airlines-cmo-network-badvocates.html?partner=email.

[40] Adam Ostrow, "Social Media Integration Drives Major Clicks for E-mail Marketers," http://mashable.com/2010/06/21/social-media-email-marketing-2/, June 21, 2010.

[41] MarketingSherpa, "New Chart: The Benefits of Sharing E-mail Content with Social Media Sites," (Warren, RI: MarketingSherpa LLC, October 27, 2009), http://www.marketingsherpa.com/article.php?ident=31425.

[42] Meredith Oliver, MIRM, President, Meredith Communications, in personal communication with the author, October 2009 and October 2010.

Glossary

analytics. Raw data available from website or blog tracking programs that note the number of unique visitors, hits, *bounce rates,* and other information.

anchor text. Clickable words in a link. Also called a *hyperlink.*

applications. Software programs that perform a specific task; commonly referred to as apps.

A record. The Internet address record, or IP address of a domain. The A record for the blog http://www. AtlantaRealEstateForum.com is the IP address 204.232.246.163.

badvocate. Advocate who uses his or her influence to spread negative information

bot. Robot that automates Internet tasks

blog. A web log, a type of website that typically focuses on one subject and displays posts in reverse chronological order.

bounce rate. The percentage of website visitors that leave a site without going further than the home page or initial landing page. A bounce can occur when a site visitor clicks on the back button or something on your site that takes them to a different site, such as your Twitter page or a special offer.

content management system (CMS). Computer systems used to control and manage data that is accessed and updated by a number of people.

Creative Commons license. A content usage license whereby the owner keeps the copyright but allows others to copy and distribute the work as long as the user credits the originator and conforms to other specific guidelines

cascading style sheet (CSS). A design and formatting tool used to define how various elements of web pages should display.

customer relationship management (CRM). A system or software to track and manage companies' inter-actions with consumers

cyberstalker. A person who uses the Internet to discover information about another individual and uses the information to cause harm by threats, accusations, or other means.

dateline. The date of your press release and the city and state from which the news originates

direct messaging (DM). A method of messaging another Twitter user, similar to an e-mail message. To DM, add a D and a space before a Twitter user's name to send the tweet directly that user.

Dots per inch (DPI). A measure of digital file resolution. The higher the number, the better the image resolution is of the file.

e-blast. An e-mail message sent to a large group of people

editorial calendar. A schedule of stories or blog entries created in advance to control and organize content over a period of time

elevator speech. Your company's succinct brand statement that tells who you are, what you do, and what you stand for.

fans, followers, friends. Social networking terms for people who follow you or your company on various social networking sites

four Ps. Product, price, place, and promotion.

hash tag. The pound sign (#); is used as a method for categorizing tweets on Twitter. It makes it easy to search specific subjects and track trends. Twitter can now be searched without the use of the hash tag, but many people still use it to organize content.

hexadecimal code. A number that represents a color displayed online

hyperlink. A clickable link to another Internet site; often referred to as anchor text.

Hyper Text Markup Language (HTML). A language used to build web pages that includes markup tags and angle brackets. Tags typically are used in pairs to delineate where an element, such as a paragraph or a subheading, should begin and end.

influencer. A person who holds sway over your potential buyers, including a real estate agent, vendor, or friend.

IRL. In real life

JavaScript. A programming language that enhances functionality for creating more dynamic websites

keyword. A word or phrase that directs an Internet user or a search engine to a relevant web page

Like. A button you can click on Facebook to give positive feedback to a friend about a post

list. A Twitter feature you can use to organize tweets

masthead. The title of a website that appears at the top of the page

microblog. A site that allows users to post short messages that are transmitted to others via the Internet. Twitter is a microblog.

netiquette. A contraction of network and etiquette or Internet and etiquette. It is a set of guidelines for how to conduct yourself online. Think of it as Emily Post for online users.

netweave. To connect online sites and channels to one another

online public relations (PR). Press releases with keywords posted online for visibility and search engine optimization

online sales counselor. An individual responsible for responding to web leads and interacting with potential buyers to set appointments at specific communities with the on-site agents

organic results. Search results that appear because of their relevance to the search term. They are not paid advertisements or *pay-per-click.*

pay-per-click. Internet advertising model where advertisers pay according to clicks on an ad

permission-based marketing. Marketing to prospective customers who have opted in and given consent to receive marketing materials or other information via social networking sites

plug-in. A computer application that serves to extend or interact with a web program or browser

push advertising. Communicating an advertising message to Internet users that they have not requested

referral site. A website that refers traffic to another site. The links may be organic or paid for by the destination site owner.

referral source. *See* referral site

refuseniks. Members of Gen Y who choose not to use social networking sites despite peer pressure.

relevance. Online content's pertinence or connection to a given topic

retweet (RT). Sending a tweet from another user; similar to forwarding an e-mail message.

return on investment (ROI). A measure of profitability versus the amount of money and time invested

really simple syndication (**RSS).** An easy way to distribute blog news via e-mail and Internet sites

search engine marketing (SEM). Promoting a website to the search engines using both paid ad placements and organic search or SEO

search engine optimization (SEO). Using various tools and techniques to ensure a website appears high in *organic search results* for a variety of keywords or phrases. Both on-page (on the website) and off-page (placed on other sites) content can be used to achieve SEO.

search engine results page (SERP). The page that displays when a user types a phrase into a search engine.

snark. A person who makes sarcastic comments

sociable logos. Clickable logos or icons for the various social networking and social bookmarking sites. Including these on e-newsletters and blog posts facilitates sharing.

social bookmarking. A method for storing, organizing, and sharing favorite websites by saving them to sites such as Digg, delicious, and Newsvine.

social media. Tools such as blogs, social networking websites, and social bookmarking.

social media marketing (SMM). The creation and distribution of content and messages on the Internet using social media, including blogs, wikis, forums, photo galleries, video, microblogs; social networking sites like Linkedin, Facebook, and Myspace, and social bookmarking. Anything one does to interact with others online outside the user's website.

social media optimization (SMO). Increasing a website's visibility and traffic using social media and search engines

social media policy. Guidelines for how a company and its employees interact online

social networking. Engaging others in two-way interaction by creating online communities

social sharing. Including social media links as an easy way for participants to share your e-newsletters and blog posts with their friends via their social networks

source. An entity or company distributing a press release

spammers. People and organizations who distribute unsolicited and unwanted bulk e-mail to large groups of people

sticky. A descriptive term for a website that holds the user's attention as demonstrated by the amount of time and the depth of pages they visit on a site

stream. On Twitter, all the tweets you can see on your home page. The stream shows all of your followers' tweets. Depending on how many you follow and how active they are, these can change rapidly.

tags. Keywords used in blog posts or on social networking sites typically used to help search engines find relevant content

teasers. Short punchy copy that entices the reader to read more. Teasers are often used on blogs or with e-mail marketing.

theme. The overall design of a site, including its appearance and functionality.

tracking. Studying web analytics over time to determine where site visitors come from and other patterns to inform business decisions

trolls. Individuals who post off-topic messages that are usually hurtful, controversial, or inflammatory to users on Twitter, Facebook, blogs, or other social sites.

tweet. A message posted on Twitter

uniform resource locator (URL). The address of a file or website

unique selling proposition. The particular attribute of your product or service that distinguishes you from other competing products and services.

user name. The name under which an individual's or company's tweets will appear, such as @AtlantaPR. The corresponding Twitter URL is http://Twitter.com/AtlantaPR.

web 2.0. The trend on the World Wide Web to network, interact, and collaborate, which has generated social media, social networking, and blogs.

website analytics. Systematic tracking of website visitors to a specific site to determine patterns and preferences to optimize the site

widget. A space on your blog to place a plug-in or other functionality

wiki. A database of live pages on the web that anyone can edit

WYSIWYG editor. An acronym that stands for What You See is What You Get. A visual editor interface that displays what users will see on the web page or blog when it is published. It eliminates or minimizes the need to insert coding manually.

Resources

Blog Directories

Blog directories are like online yellow pages. They create incoming links to your blog. There are hundreds of blog directories, both free and paid. Online Marketing Blog (http://www.toprankblog.com/rss-blog-directories/) has a list. Here are a few:

Best of Web (http://blogs.botw.org/)
Bloggeries (http://www.bloggeries.com/)
Blog Catalog (http://www.BlogCatalog.com)
Technorati (http://www.Technorati.com)

Free Blog Platforms

These third-party hosts allow you to set up your own blog:

Blogger (http://www.Blogger.com), Google's free platform
WordPress (http://www.WordPress.com)
Real Estate Sites Hub (http://www.RealEstate SitesHub.com), hosted by mRELEVANCE, a free blogging platform targeted to the real estate industry

Self-Hosted Blog Platforms

By installing blog software from TypePad or WordPress on your own hosting environment with a unique URL, you will create your own site and control its SEO, custom themes, applications, and other features.

TypePad (http://www.TypePad.com)
WordPress (http://www.WordPress.org)

Builder Blogs

Home Builder Blogs (http://www.newhomes section.com/blog/home-builder-blogs/2009/ 10/05/). This New Homes Section resource lists builders who blog.

Top Builder Blogs (http://www.TopBuilderBlogs. com). This new-homes-focused website provides examples of home builder and other industry blogs.

CRM Programs

Builder 1440 (http://www.builder1440.com)
BuildTopia (http://www.buildtopia.com)
Lasso (http://www.lassodatasystems.com)
Pivotal (http://www.cdcsoftware.com)
Salesforce (http://www.salesforce.com)
Sales Simplicity (http://www.salessimplicity.net)

E-mail Marketing Programs

Builder Broker News (http://www.builderbroker news.com)

ConstantContact (http://www.constantcontact. com)

iContact (http://www.icontact.com)

MailChimp (http://www.mailchimp.com)

Facebook

Networked Blogs. (http://www.Networked Blogs.com). This application allows you to netweave your blog with Facebook.

RSS Graffiti (http://www.facebook.com/RSS. Graffiti). An application that will post your blog feed to your Facebook wall.

General Social Media Sites

Mashable, the go-to site for social media news and tips: http://www.Mashable.com

mRELEVANCE regularly posts social media tips targeted to home builders and developers: http://www.mRELEVANCE.com

My Tech Opinion addresses technology in the real estate industry: http://www.MyTech Opinion.com

TechCrunch provides profiles and reviews
of Internet products and companies:
http://www.TechCrunch.com

URL Toolbox: 90+ URL Shortening Services.
A Mashable blog post that features 90
URL-shortening services: http://mashable.
com/2008/01/08/url-shortening-services/

Google Tools

Gmail (https://www.google.com/accounts/)

Google Analytics (http://www.google.com/
analytics/)

Google Insights for Search (http://www.google.com/
insights/search/#)

Google Reader (accessed via your gmail account)

Photo Sharing Sites

Most photo sharing sites have free basic memberships. Read the fine print to discover
their terms and conditions regarding commercial use.

Flickr (http://www.flickr.com)

Photo Bucket (http://www.photobucket.com)

Picasa. (http://picasa.google.com)

Zoomr (http://www.zooomr.com)

Public Relations Sites

http://www.1888pressrelease.com

http://www.24-7pressrelease.com

http://www.afly.com

http://www.atlantadaybook.com

http://www.bignews.biz

http://www.businesswire.com

http://www.clickpress.com

http://www.craigslist.com

http://www.dfw.daybooknetwork.com

http://www.dbusinessnews.com

http://www.epicpr.com

http://www.express-press-release.net

http://www.fastpitchnetworking.com

http://www.free-press-release.com

http://www.free-press-release-center.info

http://www.ideamarketers.com

http://www.i-newswire.com

http://www.information-online.com

http://www.live-pr.com/en

http://www.mediasyndicate.com

http://www.NashvilleDaybook.com

http://www.newsreleaser.com

http://www.nhdbuzz.com

http://www.openpr.com

http://www.pitchengine.com

http://www.pr.com

http://www.pr9.net

http://www.pressbooth.org

http://www.pressexposure.com

http://www.pressmethod.com

http://www.press-network.com

http://www.pressreleasecirculation.com

http://www.pressreleaseforum.com

http://www.pressreleasepoint.com

http://www.prfree.com

http://www.prfriend.com

http://www.prleap.com

http://www.prlog.org

http://www.prnewswire.com

http://www.prnewsnow.com

http://www.prunderground.com

http://www.pr-usa.net

http://www.PRWeb.com

http://www.prwindow.com

http://www.przoom.com

http://www.sbwire.com

http://www.theopenpress.com

http://www.usprwire.com

http://www.webnewswire.com

Real Estate-Focused Sites

New Homes Directory (http://www.NewHomes
Directory.com). This online directory lists
homes for sale.

Ask Carol (http://www.NHDbuzz.com/AskCarol).
This online service allows anyone in the new
homes industry to ask Carol Ruiz and Carol
Flammer questions on social media and public
relations.

NHD Buzz (http://www.NHDbuzz.com). This
website will post new homes industry press
releases free of charge.

Social Bookmarking Sites

Social bookmarking enables users to organize favorite
sites and share them with friends, fans, and followers.
There are literally hundreds of social bookmarking sites.
Some popular ones follow:

DIGG (www.Digg.com)
Delicious (http://www.delicious.com)
Mixx (http://www.mixx.com)
Newsvine (http://www.newsvine.com)
Reddit (http://www.reddit.com)

Sphinn (http://www.sphinn.com)
StumbleUpon (http://www.stumbleupon.com)
YahooBuzz (http://www.buzz.yahoo.com)

Social Media Monitoring

Google Alerts (http://www.google.com/alerts). A
free service that allows you to monitor the
latest news on your company, an industry,
or competitors.

Web Strategist (http://www.web-strategist.com/
blog/2006/11/25/companies-that-measure-
social-media-influcncc-brand/). A wcb page
that lists companies that measure social
media influence.

Social Media Policies

About.com Blogging and Social Media Policy
Sample (http://humanresources.about.com/
od/policysamplesb/a/blogging_policy.htm).
A page with sample blogging and social
media policies.

Social Media Governance (http://socialmedia
governance.com/policies.php). A database
of social media policies including those of
various public entities and corporations.

Social Media Policy Musts (http://mashable.com/
2009/06/02/social-media-policy-musts/).
This is a list of 10 items to include in a social
media policy.

Twitter Resources

The following articles contain tips for increasing your
Twitter followers by industry experts Kevin Rose,
founder of Digg and TechCrunch, and Chris Brogan:

Brogan, Chris. "Get More Twitter Followers
Today." http://www.chrisbrogan.com/
get-more-Twitter-followers-today/.

Rose, Kevin. "10 Ways to Increase Your Twitter
Followers." http://www.techcrunch.com/
2009/01/25/kevin-rose-10-ways-to-increase-
your-Twitter-followers/.

Twitter sorting applications allow users to sort tweets easily to stay in touch with friends and participate in chats,
track conversations, and monitor brand. Some of these applications can be integrated with Facebook and Myspace:

Tweet Deck (http://www.TweetDeck.com)
Seesmic (http://www.Seesmic.com)
Hoot Suite (http://www.HootSuite.com)

Twitter Support (http://twitter.zendesk.com/
portal). A "help" website for the popular
social networking site

Twitter Tools (http://thetwittertools.com). A website with 900+ Twitter tools and descriptions.

Video Resources

MetaCafe (http://www.metacafe.com)

Vimeo (http://www.vimeo.com)

YouTube (http://www.youtube.com)

Index